50 FISH TO CATCH IN YOUR LIFETIME

This is a Carlton Book

Text © John Bailey 2011
Design © Carlton Books Limited 2011

This edition published by Carlton Books Limited in 2011

Carlton Publishing Group
20 Mortimer Street
London W1T 3JW

10 9 8 7 6 5 4 3 2 1

A CIP catalogue record for this book is available from the British Library.

ISBN: 978-1-84732-743-7

Design: CBS Design Ltd
Picture research: Paul Langan
Production: Lisa Cook
Editorial: John Behan
Index: Chris Bell
Printed and bound in Dubai

50 FISH TO CATCH IN YOUR LIFETIME

John Bailey

CARLTON

CONTENTS

Chapter 2 – Sea Fishing

Chapter 3 – Game Fishing

FOREWORD by Chris Tarrant

"*John Bailey's book has made me realize both how lucky
I have been to catch the fish I have, but it's also made me
realize there's one hell of a lot for me yet to do.*"

Chris Tarrant

I love *Who Wants to Be a Millionaire* because it deals in dreams. For a small number of people, the program can change lives. And *50 Fish* can change lives, too. John and I share the same sort of views about fishing and life both. Life is a great gift. Fishing is a great sport. It's full of great variety and great opportunity. This is a great book, I think, because it sets the seeds for some of the most absorbing adventures in the angling world.

Oh no, I first thought. Not another impossible-to-achieve book by an angling celeb. I should have known better. JB is the sort of guy who speaks to everyone. This is what I like about the book most because it's inclusive. Anyone can get on *Who Wants to Be a Millionaire*. Anyone can join in on the angling race that is *50 Fish*. A total novice can kick off with a stickleback. The inexperienced can catch a perch or dace. And there are carp, barbel, and bass to come. If you are lucky in life and get the right questions, there are the romance fish to be pursued. Tarpon. Marlin. Mahseer. Even Beluga sturgeon. 50 Fish? You could spend 50 years following the dream.

There is technique in the book. Great photographs, too. And I love the illustrations. But it's the adrenaline of aspiration that keeps you turning the pages. I like John because he loves any and every fish, and that's apparent in the way he describes everything that swims from golden rudd to golden dorado. These are descriptions of fish and fishing that will drive you to get out there. *50 Fish* is an armchair book to a degree but one of the few that will force you to leave it for the bankside. That's what it's done to me. I've had a pretty full fishing life, and I was content with it until *50 Fish* came my way. John Bailey's book has made me realize both how lucky I have been to catch the fish I have, but it's also made me realize there's one hell of a lot for me yet to do. Yes, *50 Fish* has got me thinking and planning and looking forward to my fishing future as I haven't done for years.

Chris Tarrant, 2008.

INTRODUCTION *by John Bailey*

Man I say from the outset that all fish are magnificent? It's hard to think of a single fish I've ever seen that hasn't been perfectly formed, perfectly beautiful, and perfectly desirable. Choosing 50, therefore, to create a list has involved me in all sorts of arbitrary and subjective decisions. So, if you look at the list and you groan with dismay because I've omitted your particular favorite, please try to sympathize. Almost certainly, your pal won't be on the list simply because I haven't met up with him. What I've tried to do, as often as possible, is include characters that I've personally tangled with in some way. Wherever possible, I've just tried to make it personal. Of course, there are some fish in the list that are just beyond my ken and I've had to rely on accounts given to me by close and special friends. That way, though secondhand, they've really come alive for me, and I hope you.

Scratching my head over this, I suppose subconsciously what I've tried to do is choose fish that fit one of five categories. First, there are fish in the list that give most of us the opportunity to catch them. I think this is important. If all the fish were wildly exotic, how would so many of us even begin to tick them off? So, you might be a lad on a bicycle. Or a hard-working family man, pressed for time. The chance of sailing the Azores on a big game boat is pretty remote. But, however, you do stand a chance of a roach, a dace, or a stickleback. For that reason alone, these accessible species sail into the 50. And always remember, in my book, a stickleback is just as sensational as a salmon.

Secondly, there are those fish that become available to us as our experience grows and, perhaps, we become a little more mobile. Perhaps now we can look at catching a black bass, a sea bass, or a barbel. The third group of fish in the 50 are those that excite our ambition. With a few years fishing under our belt and a certain amount of success, we can now begin to set out sights a bit higher, at species that are glamorous but are well within the realms of possibility. A steelhead, for example, or perhaps a sea trout.

The fourth selection from the 50 represents a dream. A goal to be aimed for. A fish that will only be won after huge endeavour. Perhaps we're talking about a sturgeon or a mahseer or a taimen or even a muskellunge. Catch any one of this category of species and you can retire an angler who has been blessed.

And then, fifthly, right at the extreme end of the list, we have the impossible dreams. The two most obvious examples of these are the Goliath tiger fish and the arapaima. Their rarity and their remoteness take them far out of the reach of all of us who are at least partly sane. A Mekong catfish would be another such customer, rare as a coelacanth!

The title of this book is *50 Fish to Catch before You Die*. Actually, if you want to know the truth, that's a bit of a misnomer for me. For many years, my own fishing mantra has become the simple phrase, 'Being there.' For me, today, and certainly for the past 15 years, it's enough to witness a major angling event. If I'm there to watch a splendid fish caught, it's just as good as catching it myself. In fact, because I've got so many dear fishing friends that I enjoy seeing happy, it's frequently better. Believe me, if you adopt this approach, you get the two monkeys of greed and jealousy off your back and your angling becomes much more pleasurable in the future. Share genuinely in the triumph of others and you will get all manner of unexpected rewards.

I'm an avid birder as well as fisherman and there are similarities. I enjoy seeing a bittern or an albatross or whatever and ticking them off my list. It's the same with fish. Just to see my first Arctic char is an event I will never forget. Mind you, seeing my first perch when I was four years old was just as memorable. So, again, you see that Catching isn't really as important as Seeing.

I've enjoyed putting this book together enormously. It's been a labor but one of immense love. Who can grumble over writing about what one loves the most? I've been collecting fishing books since I could read and now, as I write, I'm absolutely surrounded by them. They've been my constant friends, inspirations, and treasure troves of information for these past months. So, too, my diaries. I have scores of them, mostly written during various fishing expeditions around the world. As I've leafed through them I'd forgotten so many friends, places, events, and fish. Revisiting them all has been a pleasure. I realize I have hundreds of people to thank, people who have made my fishing life so rich and privileged. First and foremost, though, I must thank Matt Lowing of Carlton Books who commissioned this work and gave me the opportunity to delve back into the most precious moments of my angling past…and to let me dream about adventures with fabulous fish still to come.

CHAPTER 1
BAIT FISHING

STICKLEBACK *Gasterosteus family*

The Magic of the First

Region: North America, Europe, Siberia

"In many ways, it is a mercy that sticklebacks do not grow very large. Like the shrew on land, they are tiny but ferocious. I saw one once kept in a tank with a two pound roach that it bullied mercilessly. After a few days, they had to be separated."

Dr Stephen Knowles, The New Complete Angler 1983.

Target length:	3 inches
Dream length:	4 inches
Areas:	Worldwide
Food:	Invertebrates

SUMMARY
Small and pugnacious, sticklebacks can exist in heavily brackish water. Their diet consists of small invertebrates.

When listing the top 50 you can't neglect the stickleback. When you think about it, they probably gave us the best days of our lives, those days when everything was new, fresh, and thrilling. Remember that first time the float bobbed? The magic of the first chewed worm? The first successful strike? The momentary feel of a living, wriggling creature connected to you by a line as vital as an umbilical cord. There it is quivering in a net, shimmering in the sunlight, skipping in the palm of your hand. Your fish. No tiddler. Your achievement.

If you live in North America, perhaps your tiddler is a blue gill, a pumpkin seed, or a crappy. If you live on the coast, it might be a sprat, a sand eel, or even a crab. If you live on a European river, perhaps you've caught an iron-blue gudgeon with cornflower fins. If they grew to three pounds instead of three ounces, none of us would have ever fished for anything else.

You ought to know that the UK gudgeon record is a mighty four ounces. It's been that weight for eons and it certainly was in 1987, when Roger and I spotted a leviathan gudgeon beneath a road bridge on the River Wensum in Norfolk. We found him one late May afternoon when we were watching for roach spawning on the shallows where he lived. There were big roach about, colossal roach in fact, but it was only the gudgeon that we had eyes for. He dwarfed his compatriots. Conservatively, we put him at six ounces, one and a half times the record. Privately, we reckoned that he doubled it. The fishing season, though, wasn't due to begin for nearly three weeks. We just had to bide our time, wait and pray that he didn't move on.

We checked him daily, right up to the dawn of June 16th when we could legitimately fish for him. We baited him carefully, dribbling in maggots throughout our visits until he was taking them with confidence. This would be a pushover. And we were well prepared. We'd bought an intricate, new weighing machine that could measure to within slivers of an ounce. We had tape measures, too, and cameras and everything we could think of to record our triumph.

In the event, he was wiser than we thought. Frequently he would approach our hooked maggot and shy away. We caught plenty of his shoal members but they were pinheads by comparison. Then, at last, our float sank. He was on. He struggled wildly. So bullish he seemed, I was tempted to give line. But, in fact, he came to the net quite quickly. I remember the giddying excitement as we looked at him, massive in the meshes. Huge. We levered him onto the waiting scales. Three and a quarter ounces.

It could not be. We weighed him again. We weighed him on different scales. We jiggled the scales. No way could we even approach the quarter pound mark. Personally, after this, I can't even begin to think what a record gudgeon would look like. A whale probably.

Being born in the industrial part of northern England, I had to make do with canals, those bleak waterways that had helped propel the Industrial Revolution – if propel is the right word for a barge full of coal pulled by a plodding horse. There was one place in particular that captured my infant imagination, near a textile mill that perennially piled smoke and fumes into the air and dye and dirt into the water. Not a great deal survived under that sheen of oil, but sticklebacks did. And they were wonderful. Sharp nosed. Silver plated. Spikes bristling. Pectorals never still. Males robin-red at spawning time – how fine they looked in a two pound jar as they hovered and darted to peck their reflection in the glass. To me, aged four, they were giants of fish. Perhaps a big female would have been two inches long and weighed the most part of an ounce.

It's been many years since I went to the north. I guess the pits and ponds we used to fish are long since covered over by industrial and housing estates. The mill is probably a smart development for Manchester business executives now that there is little demand for looms in Lancashire. Do their children, I wonder, hunt the descendents of those sticklebacks I so carefully emptied back after their time in the jar?

STICKLEBACK FACTS

• The stickleback is an aggressive species. Males are especially so at spawning time when they construct a nest and chase off all intruders upon their eggs and newly-hatched fry.

• Sticklebacks have the extraordinary ability to lock their pectoral and dorsal fins in place. This means that when a predator grabs them they can sometimes be faced with a wall of sharp, impossible-to-swallow fins. An advantage in the struggle for life in the kingdom of the minis.

August, 1998. The Qorqut River, southwest Greenland.

It's been many years since I've thought much about sticklebacks at all. Today changes all that. Simon and I leave our tented camp soon after breakfast to make it to the top pools before the sun rises high and hot. It's a serious hike, at least two hours hard walking before you get to the fringes of the heaven that is the fishing here. In the penultimate pool there are rows of fresh-run Arctic char and I leave Simon whilst I plough to the top-most holding water beneath the unscaleable waterfall.

There, I catch two great, silver char and watch them glisten in the bright Greenlandic light. I wonder how it is my life has been so fortunate, how fish have guided it to breathtaking valleys like this one. Apart from the river's voice, I'm in a world of complete silence looking out over a beauty that has not altered for millennia and probably never will in the eternity to come.

And now I have this thought. Suppose super char manage to ride the waterfall? Just perhaps somewhere towards the Ice Cap there are monsters to rival or surpass those I found in Paradise Valley. After two hours of struggle, I realise there are not. The Qorqut has revealed all its secrets. But what's that? Way across the tundra, there's a lake of about four acres standing in the shelter of an ice cliff. In half an hour I'm there. It's crystal, like an ice cube the size of a mountain has melted. Like the purest rains falling through the most uncontaminated skies in the world have all gathered here. And there are fish rising. Even in this teardrop water I can't make them out, though.

I cast out a large, artificial fly a reservoir lure and strip it back. It's pecked at. I can feel it being tugged but it's not being taken. Cast after cast, I keep reducing the size of my fly until, on a size 16 nymph, I'm taken solidly. The fly line doesn't strip, merely tremors. I swing to hand a small, silvery, struggling fish. Then I realize it is a MONSTER. Yes, it's a stickleback but a huge, goliath stickleback. It's quite five inches long. It must be near three times the size of anything I've seen before with spines. It must weigh an ounce and a half. I slip it back but I sorely wish I had a jam jar.

TENCH *Tinca tinca*

A Lesson in Loveliness

Region: Europe and Asia

"The cooing of doves, the hum of bees, and all the pageantry of high summer seem somehow to be recalled by the word 'tench'. Perhaps it is that fish invites meditation."

H. T. Sheringham An Angler's Hours.

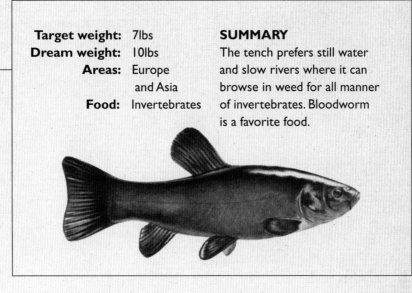

Target weight:	7lbs	
Dream weight:	10lbs	
Areas:	Europe and Asia	
Food:	Invertebrates	

SUMMARY

The tench prefers still water and slow rivers where it can browse in weed for all manner of invertebrates. Bloodworm is a favorite food.

There are just so many delights to our sport. Take the tench. The tench cruises into the 50 list through its gentleness. You're not talking a toothy barracuda here or some mean, cold-eyed predator. The tench is a browser, a lover of the summer and warm water. That's one of its appeals. Think tench and you think of summer. Misty, milky-warm dawns. Golden sunsets that signal the end of another perfect day. Tench, too, are perfect in their understated way. Look at their olive-green sides. Their little, penetrating, red eyes. Their scales smooth as silk. Their rounded, chocolate colored fins. There's nothing angular about a tench, they're all curvy, all cuddly. Sweet as honey.

But as I say, best of all about the tench is where it lives and how you catch it. You can catch tench throughout Europe, but they are at their best in an English estate lake. Most of these were built in the 18th century during the golden age of the country house and they remain, many of them, as little oases of paradise in an overcrowded island. Most of these estate lakes hold tench and many were stocked over 200 years ago with the species. It's good to think that generation upon generation of tench have lived and thrived into the modern day. These are serene places to fish. There will probably be clock towers with a peal of bells chiming away the hours. You might approach the lake through a walled garden or over formal lawns. The lake might be in a deer park. There will be woods, probably boathouses, islands, and a twinkling stream running from the dam. Gorgeous. It's like casting back a whole century.

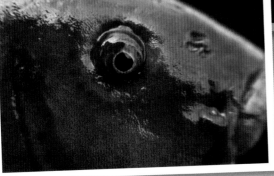

A tench fights well but it's not a fight to frighten you. Enjoy it. A happy five minutes. The rod bends and the reel shrieks but you've got a smile on your face. And then, just look at the fish. So unique. So pleasing to the eye. You lay it on the weeds and it's just green on green. It's all quintessentially English countryside and summertime.

You might well decide to fish from the dam where the water is just that little bit deeper. Out goes your ground bait, a sprinkling of corn perhaps, or half a bucket of mashed bread. With luck, soon, you'll see tight clusters of small, pinhead, fizzing bubbles rise to the surface. You'll be using a float – you've almost got to for tench if you're going to maintain the atmosphere. It will be a red float, too, probably a quill. You'll set it just a little bit over the depth so it's lying on the surface, half-cocked. It will stir every now and again as a tench brushes past. It will rise, rock, sway and there'll be minutes of action before it gathers pace and slides away.

TENCH FACTS

• The tench is one of the few species of fish very easy to sex. The key is in the pelvic fins. The males' are longer and broader than those of the female and they extend noticeably beyond the anal vent.

• Tench are almost always fish of warm weather. In the northern hemisphere, they begin to feed as spring warms the water and taper off as autumn bites. They're occasionally caught in winter during very mild or flood conditions.

July 2006. The Deer Park Lake, England.

For several reasons, for a quarter of a century, the Deer Park Lake has been off the angling map, completely forbidden to all anglers. Neill Stephen knows that single fact is going to be a problem for him. The tench won't be scared of tackle, that's true, but neither will they recognize bait. Tench aren't particularly curious fish in the manner of carp and they will have become used to browsing on bloodworm and slurping in daphnia. The Deer Park is a hugely rich lake and the tench will have no need to investigate any unusual foodstuffs. And, as I've already said, they're conservative fish. They know their own mind. They settle into a pleasing routine. Neill knows there isn't a huge amount of chance that he will break them out of their rut. Neill doesn't even know if there are tench left in the lake. Otters and cormorants, both, are their enemies and, with no fishing pressure or knowledge, the lake has become an enigma.

He decides two things. He will get there just before first light and watch the lake minutely for any sign of moving fish. Secondly, he's going to bait heavily with maggots. At least maggots do look a little like a natural foodstuff, the sort of tiny, wriggling creature that could live in the lake. He's going to float fish on a ledge where the water drops from five to eight feet deep. This very probably will be a patrol route for any tench that are still in existence. Five a.m. and the mist is rising in a great, grey, silent blanket from the water's surface. The far bank and the hall across the meadows are completely obscured. Six a.m. The mist miraculously clears as the sun gains some strength and, far out, a big fish swirls. Neill caught only the end of the disturbance, though, and has no clue as to the culprit. It could easily be a pike or even a carp.

Seven a.m. Suddenly, without any warning, Neill's red float rises half an inch in the water and tremors. Neill is by his rod in an instant but the minutes tick by and the float simply settles into its original position and doesn't move again. Certainly, this slow, subtle movement is tench like but it could easily have been caused by a small perch or roach attacking the bait or even pecking at the shot on the line. Eight a.m. Suddenly, two patches of bubbles appear in the vicinity of Neill's float. They're quite sustained and last for a couple of minutes each. The bubbles look right. They're small, closely packed, fizzing and very, very tenchy. Okay, not proof positive by any stretch of the imagination but Neill is hopeful.

Nine a.m. This is the moment. In frozen time, in slow motion, a tench porpoises out of the water just to the left of Neill's float. It's a graceful, soundless movement. You see the tench's head, its back, its dorsal fin and finally, its disappearing tail. And it was a big fish. Neill senses that he is close. Ten a.m. The float disappears. There are no preliminaries. It's just gone. There's no huge drama about the fight but it lasts and it lasts. The fish is heavy and it bores again and again down towards the lake bed, pulling the 12 foot rod over into a complete hoop. Great boils churn on the surface as the fish comes into mid-water and at 10 minutes past 10, Neill nets a glorious tench. It's just ounces short of nine pounds. The Deer Park Lake is still alive.

ROACH *Rutilus rutilus*

The Pearl of Nature

Region: Europe, Asia, Scandinavia

"That roach are gentle, no one would deny. They are the most serene of all our coarse fish. They graze the underwater world with all the calm of horses at pasture. Look into the eye of an 18-year-old roach and you have an insight into a wisdom that has accepted disease, droughts, and pike attacks with stoic resignation. When such a fish dies, the river bed receives it and day by day covers it in the finest silt, whilst the alders and the willows wish it farewell."

From Roach, the Gentle Giants *John Bailey, 1987.*

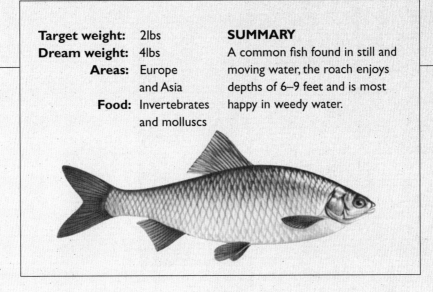

Target weight: 2lbs
Dream weight: 4lbs
Areas: Europe and Asia
Food: Invertebrates and molluscs

SUMMARY
A common fish found in still and moving water, the roach enjoys depths of 6–9 feet and is most happy in weedy water.

I'm not sure that anywhere else in the world the roach is as treasured as it is here in England. In Scotland, it's treated as a pest because it interferes with the spawning beds of trout and salmon. Wales doesn't have many roach at all, and in Ireland they're regarded a bit as an intruder. I've watched Frenchmen fish very sensitively for roach on the River Seine under the bridges of Paris. They appear to admire them. I fished with a German miller once who caught a big roach from his pool – it was probably a kilo – and we celebrated long into the night with beer and sausages.

I once caught a massive roach – well over four pounds – in the south of Austria. The local anglers gathered round me and there was much back-slapping. Once again, beer was produced. I think I remember going back to a café with two of them at the end of the day.

I later checked the photographs with the textbooks and I suspect my roach wasn't a true *rutilus rutilus* but, in fact, a Danubian roach. They're not quite the same thing but it doesn't alter the fact that the Austrians seem to value a roach.

So what is it about roach? True, they're not particularly large and they don't fight particularly hard. But they are cunning. And they are serene. And best of all, they can be stunningly beautiful. If you catch a big roach from a rich river, I guarantee it's as beautiful a fish as you'll ever meet with. The scales aren't quite blue, or silver, or pearl, but a bewildering mix of all three. The fins are an exquisite shade of red that you won't see on any other living creature. In the water when it's clear and when the sun is shining, they're so gorgeous that, for this moment, you can forget any other fish that swims.

holding these monsters of fish that looked as though they'd come from the moon.

Then, as a teenager, I found my own mega roach. My parents moved me to Norfolk and one night in January, sitting under an alder tree, I hauled out a roach of two pounds 14 ounces. That's 46 ounces. Consider that until this moment a roach of eight ounces appeared enormous and you will grasp the scale of my elation.

For many, many years thereafter, I fished these Norfolk rivers at dusk and into the night. I always fished the same way. I'd find a bend. I'd fish a lump of bread hard on the bed of the river. I'd sit watching an indicator on the line, praying that it would twitch and then move relentlessly up towards the rod butt. I caught hundreds of two pounders. I caught several over three. Year by year, success by success, the longings of my childhood were satisfied.

And there was something magical about those nights. The misty, mysterious marshes, the call of the owl. The cough of the fox. And above all, those great, massive fish lying there before me in the torchlight. But, you see, fishing like that is not quite the way that you should catch roach. If you are going to catch a big roach before you die, then you've got to do it right. You've got to trot a float. It's got to be the daylight so you can see what you're doing, truly appreciate the glory of what you catch. I appreciate all this now. It's not what you catch but how you catch it that counts.

The French, the Germans, and the Austrians might like their roach but here, in England, they're kings. I was brought up with northern match men who worshipped roach. These weren't big roach by any means – a four ounce fish was revered – but they were still exquisite in their own way. And, in the cold, thin, clear, gruelling waters of the industrial north, they were nerve-rackingly difficult to catch. As a kid, they were beyond me. I used to watch my heroes swinging in these silver giants and gawp. Of course, to these men, each fish increased their chances of a win and then, not that long after the war, money thereabouts was tighter than you can imagine. To take home just a pound or two made a difference. Roach then, to them, were almost like shiny, silver, little coins. Of course, as I grew older, I learned to catch roach myself. I found that if I got on my bike and cycled way, way out into the countryside where the fish were less suspicious, I stood a better chance. Sometimes, I even caught a big roach or two and I'd cycle home, my heart bursting.

Even then I knew that there was a different type of roach. Down in the south of England, in Wessex, where the rivers were bigger and richer and weed growth was abundant, there swam roach of two pounds, even three. These were eight, even 10 times larger than anything we might expect to catch in the north. They were caught by heroes like Owen Wentworth, the postman from Dorset. His catches were legendary. I used to see his photograph in the press

ROACH FACTS

• The age of fish is something that has always fascinated me. Traditionally, it was believed that roach, in favorable circumstances, could grow for between 9 and 11 or 12 years, and then fairly soon peaked and died. This doesn't make sense to me. It's like suggesting that human beings grow until they're about 18 and die in their early 20s. Even before poor medicine, we could make it to our 50s or 60s and I think it's the same with roach. My own recaptures of big, recognizable fish over the years suggests that roach at least have a lifespan of 20 years.

February 2008. The River Wensum, England.

It's not a bad sort of day. There's fitful, feathery sunshine and a breeze that's sharp but not biting. The air temperature is, I guess, eight or nine degrees Celsius which is good, too. And the river runs nicely, with a tinge of color but you can see easily at least two feet down. A memory stirs within me. I remember back 32 years to a morning much like this. Then, though, it was Saturday and I was fishing with a long-time friend. We were in exactly this place, above a mill, where the river runs steady, straight and deep. That morning we caught 400 roach!! They came in every size from two ounces to two ounces under three pounds. It was the best day's roach fishing I've ever enjoyed.

During these 30 years, though, the Wensum isn't the roach river it was. Insidious agricultural and industrial pollutions, abstraction and above all, injurious drainage policies increasingly damaged the roach habitat. For years, the species has been hanging on. It's only recently that there's ever been any real hope of a revival. That's why I'm here. I've got a lot of hope in my heart.

Today, I'm roaching the right way. A 14 foot rod. Center pin reel. Beautiful red-tipped stick float. A bucket of maggots and I'm trotting the run of river beneath me. This is the way to fish for roach. Out go a handful of maggots and I swing the float gently into the river behind them. The trot begins.

Perhaps I'm not a real artist, one of the true experts, but I'm still finding what I do exquisite. Controlling that float at range so it moves exactly as it should, not too fast, not too slow, never dragging across the current is a physical skill that I'm relishing. That wind gives everything a spice. It's constantly trying to blow the float off course so I have to work a little harder, fish with a bit more intelligence. For two hours, I don't see a sign of a roach but I'm not really bothered. The fishing itself is absorbing. Each trot I try to make better than the one that preceded it. I feel like my skills are being honed, time after time.

It's probably two thirty in the afternoon when IT happens. At 40 yards range, the float holds up a second and dives under. I sweep the rod back and there's a sort of clunk as the pressure bites in. The rod tip goes round and there's something alive and throbbing in the current. Of course, it's not a white-knuckle fight but that doesn't mean my heart doesn't stop when I see a good roach rolling just out from my net. It's not a monster. It's not two pounds. But it's probably only five or six ounces under that. It's big enough for me. It shows there are roach on the way back which is good. And I caught it the right way which is great.

CHUB *Leuciscus cephalus*

The Greediest Fish

Region: Europe, excluding Ireland, and much of Scandinavia

"Funny day on River Trent. Alan and I thought we'd play a trick on old George. It was his eightieth birthday. He always falls asleep at the start of the match and wakes up at the end saying 'Not A Sausage'. Thought this time we'd reel in his gear and put a sausage on. Fast asleep he was. An easy job to do. Alan and I go round with the scales and George is awake for the first time, walking up and down the bank. All excited. Seems he reeled in and there was this bloomin' great chub on the end. It had eaten our sausage! Alan would have won the match but for that."

From John Bailey's fishing diary, England, September 1961.

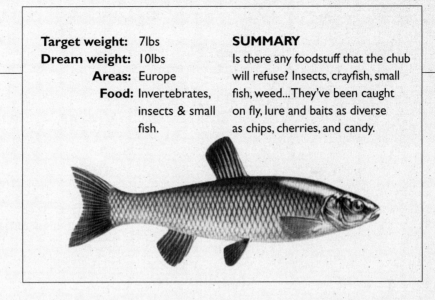

Target weight: 7lbs
Dream weight: 10lbs
Areas: Europe
Food: Invertebrates, insects & small fish.

SUMMARY
Is there any foodstuff that the chub will refuse? Insects, crayfish, small fish, weed...They've been caught on fly, lure and baits as diverse as chips, cherries, and candy.

The lesson of George's chub is that the species is the tummy boy of the 50. It doesn't matter how cold or how hot the water, the chub will oblige. If you've got to get a bite to save your life, the chub is your get out of jail card. High or low, colored or clear, fast or slow, deep or shallow, a river can be any way it wants and chub will have a go. It's like they're on a permanent food fest. They're never quite full enough. Yum-yum, there's always room for one titbit more.

I once had an old mill house situated on the banks of an English lowland river. The window of the sitting room looked out onto a half-decent chub swim and, one spring afternoon, there was a good fat chub in situ. I knew him quite well and put his weight at almost four pounds. A nice, bold, brassy fish. There happened to be some cheese in the fridge, an exactly weighed pound of cheddar. I broke him off a piece and lobbed it into the water. It was engulfed. So were the next 30 pieces. In fact, the entire pound disappeared into his big, white, rubbery-lipped mouth. He even finished off with a couple of slices of crusty brown bread. Within an hour, that fish had eaten around 25 percent of its own body weight. It's rather like a 12 stone man chomping through a three stone lunch.

Despite this considerable appetite, chub are not stupid. That's what makes them so beguiling. They never stop eating, but equally, they're never easy to fool. You can catch a chub once easily. If you're lucky enough to land on a virgin piece of water then they'll take just about anything. I remember some stretches of river where I've caught 40 fish with ease in an afternoon. You go back the second day expecting similar sorts of success. You struggle to catch two or three.

In my life, I've met up with several chub that I've come to know well. It's been my firm belief that these fish have been totally and utterly uncatchable under normal circumstances. You might just fool them by fishing into the dead of night. They might make a mistake if the river colors up as brown as coffee. You might just hoodwink them by scaling down to gossamer light gear – but there's no point in that because you'd lose them the instant they were hooked.

That's what happened when I tangled with Moby Dick. Moby was the fabled, huge, ivory-skinned chub that dominated my local river back in the 1970s. Many saw and desired him. Nobody, that I'm aware, actually caught him. Often he would be in public view, but it was like he knew it. Some of the best fishing talents of that period pursued him without a sniff of success. So Mr. Scientist never tell me that chub have a brain the size of a pea and the memory span of seconds.

My nearest brush with Moby came one sunny summer afternoon when he positively glowed with desirability. I fed in maggots for two hours until he was quite delirious over them. His tummy must have been a squirming ball before I put my own bait before him. A single maggot on a tiny hook to line the breaking strain of a hair. He engulfed the maggot without a second thought and I set the hook. At leisurely pace, Moby went downstream, into the overhanging willow and the hook pulled free. That's how I fooled Moby…or, in truth that's how I fooled myself.

Another reason chub make the 50 is the fact that not only do they eat most things on the planet they can be caught by most methods on the planet too.

CHUB FACTS

When chub are adult, there appear to be two slightly differing sub-species. One type of chub exhibits silvery scales and well-colored, reddish fins. The second type favours brassy scales and fins more black than red. Very big chub can be highly nomadic. Angling pressure can move them miles, so can the presence of a working otter. Smaller shoal chub tend to be more territorial. Chub, interestingly, spend a great deal of time actually under the marginal weed beds in any river. They probably do this hunting for food and also looking for sanctuary.

March, 2008. The River Wensum, Norfolk, England.

It's a bright, mild, nearly spring-like day. The end of the river fishing season isn't far off and, unexpectedly, I've got half a day to myself. Only one thing to do "Go a-chubbing."

I'm at the head of a long, straight, intriguing run of water. I guess it's 120 yards to the far bend and all the way along there are overhanging trees, making this a veritable tunnel of chub. I'm mixing up mashed bread and throwing a few handfuls in. It will sink very, very slowly giving a curtain effect as it drops downriver. Perfect. A 14 foot trotting rod, four pound main line, a bulky Avon float, a size six hook yes, a six! And a big lump of flake and I'm ready to rock 'n' roll.

The float weaves its merry way 10 yards, 20 yards, 40 yards and, just on the 80 yard mark it dips, curtseys and vanishes. I strike steadily, firmly and far, far back over my right shoulder. There's a thump and the fish is on. It's five pounds of brassy beauty.

Now I'm a bit lower down the river where there are more bends and, because it's a little shallower, I can nearly see the bottom. I've got a fly rod in my hands a six-weight with a small surface popper of a fly tied on. It's the fly, actually, I use in Spain for black bass. Fourth cast, a chub comes up to investigate. It follows the popper two yards upstream before vanishing. I move on. Just above the mill, first cast, the popper is taken on the charge. I've only twitched it the once when the shape comes up behind it, the head rears over it and I'm into a second fish of three and a half pounds.

Now I'm in what we call the Jungle, a dark piece of water where trees overhang forming rafts on the surface, with deep, shady pools beneath. I'm flicking out bits of cheese, watching them waft their way to the bottom. Quite a few are taken on the drop, in mid-water by chub of a size that doesn't interest me. I'm looking for a biggie. After four to five minutes and a pound of cheese, I find him. He's tight in the sunken branches of an old alder, ripped off by a winter storm. I feed him four pieces of cheese, pulling him further and further away from his cover. He's hungry now. He's on the prowl, looking for more of the white stuff.

An Avon rod, five pound line and a big ball of cheese on that size six hook and in it goes with a splash. He hears and he's attracted and opens his mouth and he's mine. Three fine chub on three fascinating methods.

RUDD

Scardinius erythrophthalmus

The Sovereign Scaled Beauty

Region: Most of Europe and Asia

"The man said it was a golden rudd. It weighed six and a half ounces and it was yellow like buttercups rather than gold. Its fins were absolutely red and its eye was yellow, too. I think it's the prettiest fish that I have ever seen. I think these are wonderful and I would like to catch a lot more."

From John Bailey's fishing diary, A Pool in Cheshire, England, 1959.

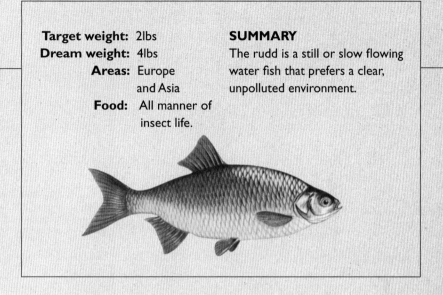

Target weight: 2lbs
Dream weight: 4lbs
Areas: Europe and Asia
Food: All manner of insect life.

SUMMARY
The rudd is a still or slow flowing water fish that prefers a clear, unpolluted environment.

All those years ago, I was correct. Rudd sail into the 50 on their coloring alone. It's not that they are big particularly, or glamorously shaped, or fight much but they are so gobsmackingly beautiful that you can never, ever conceive of tiring of them. Are they the most beautiful fish that swims? Without doubt of the cyprinids, they've got to be close.

And, appallingly, they're tragically overlooked. Another reason to include them here. Today, with the European attitude that bigger is best, these gems of fish, these veritable scaled sovereigns, are in danger of extinction.

That's not too strong a word. In my lifetime, I've known one rudd water after another collapse. Cormorants haven't helped and nor have otters. Rudd are fish of ponds and shallow pools – so frequently filled in and built over by encroaching developments. And, above all, rudd are gentle fish. They don't swagger about bullying other species. They are the ones bullied. Especially by carp. Without doubt, the spread of the ubiquitous mirror carp has been a major reason that rudd have fallen on hard times. If a club has a stillwater now, they stock it with carp. Rudd, tragically, just don't get a look in. I'm told that one country where rudd still thrive as ever before is Holland. I'm not surprised. The Dutch show sense in most things.

Most of my rudd fishing has taken place on estate lakes in the East of England. These waters were generally created 200 years or so ago and stocked with fish brought from the nearby Norfolk Broads where rudd always predominated. They were brought on carts and carried in wooden tanks and buckets and flourished in the rich, shallow waters.

There's one lake I know where there are huge rudd. They come close to the dam wall at dusk and you can get them onto the surface to feed there on scraps of floating bread. They're magnificent. They cloop and they slurp as the warm summer night edges in. Sometimes, you see their great golden heads come clear of the water as they gobble in a particularly juicy crust. Their dorsal fins glow sparklingly red in what's left of the light.

During the day, you'll find them at the far end of the lake in the reed beds and just sometimes, they'll intercept sprinkled maggots as they waft down through the water column. But rudd are never still, they're always spooky. They'll probably suck in two or three maggots at most and then become wary and eventually melt into nothingness, the anonymity of the night.

I'm a fortunate man in that I have enjoyed wondrous rudd fishing in my life and another reason I place them so highly in the 50 list is because nearly all rudd fishing is sight fishing. You know, the more I think about it, I can't think of a good rudd water that is cloudy. Classic rudd waters are always crystal clear. It's as though the species demands it. That's what makes some of the Irish loughs so utterly tantalizing. You can ease your boat for hour upon hour around the reed margins on a hot, sunny day, peering into water like glass. You'll have your Polaroids on of course and you'll travel at the speed of a snail with absolutely no splash from the oars. If you're lucky – and it's a sight to remember – you will come across a group of rudd. There might be up to 20 of them. One or two might just top three pounds. You'll see them there, glinting golds and reds in the sunlight. You can be so stunned that you nearly forget to cast. You will have one chance, two at the most, before they sprint off in tight unison almost like starlings settling to roost for the night. You pray you land one fish. It might be two and a half pounds. It's more beautiful than anything you've seen anywhere in the world.

RUDD FACTS

Over much of Europe, the rudd has been muscled out over the past 40 years because of stockings with the ubiquitous mirror carp. Also, it has frequently hybridized with roach. When the roach got into Ireland, for example, the days of the true rudd, in many places, were numbered. Of course, you can ask if it really matters whether a fish is a true this or a true that and you'd be right that hybrids are very worth catching in their own right. They often grow big and are frequently very beautiful. Yet, it's vital we maintain our pure stocks of fish where they are threatened.

June 2003. Castle Lake, England.

To the north, there's a high bank and the just-risen sun is streaming into the shallows beneath me. I instantly see the bigger of the two fish as it turns slightly to intercept a hatching insect. The sun's rays bounce off its scales as though the fish were a shield. This is a massive rudd. The question. Do I fish a nymph or a dry? Just to catch a fish like this, I think, off the top is well worth the gamble. I look round the nearby hedgerow and, in the webs of countless spiders, I see the corpses of small sedges and olives. And it's an olive I tie on, a size 14, a perfect mouthful for this goddess of a fish.

Both fish are intent on feeding just underneath the surface and I land the fly like thistledown six or so inches shy of them with barely a ripple. They're both instantly aware of its appearance. You can see that by the way they tilt, by the way they glide with purpose towards it. But though they see the fly, they don't want it. Perhaps it's too big. Perhaps they see the line. What's sure is that they're moving off.

Now, I'm putting a small epoxy red buzzer to them. I've greased the leader so it's hanging just a couple of inches under the surface. The smaller fish — I say smaller but that's three pounds — approaches. I think it has taken. I'm not sure. Yes. The leader twitches. I lift. The fish rolls. It's colossal. The rod tip thumps. And it's gone. There is a swirl of water as the two fish disappear off into the deep, central channel. I'm devastated.

I look along the reed beds. I see nothing but tench. I inch my way round the island where the water is a mere foot deep. There's nothing. I move down the woody bank, climbing every tree I can to see into the dark water beneath. And here there are rudd. Big rudd. Several rudd. I watch one group and work out my strategy. Their patrol route, every 10 minutes or so, brings them into open water where I can make a cast. I tie on a shrimp pattern and I sit back to wait.

It's a wonderful day. There are kingfishers busy and damselflies, just as vibrantly blue. A tench wanders past chewing on its breakfast of bloodworms. And the rudd are here. Seven of them. All two pounders. I'll have one cast. This is crucial, critical.

The shrimp goes in with a plop. Is it too heavy? No. A rudd peels off and accelerates. It's gone. I resist the urge to strike too soon and wait until the leader pulls tight. Then I pull into the fish steadily, slowly but firmly. The rudd is rocked. I pull it off balance. It rights itself and heads ominously towards a fallen tree. I'm only using a four-weight but it's enough. Just. I turn the rudd inches away from the branches. Two more attempts and it rolls, beaten on the surface, mine. My glorious fish of the morning.

DACE *Leuciscus leuciscus*

The Silver Dart

Region: Northern Europe from Ireland to Siberia

"The flood plain was frozen into icing as far as the eye could see and whilst the sun was still up, the frost coated hard on the rod and the line glued itself to the rings. The birds were already in the bare-bone wood – everything else had burrowed in for a dire night – when I caught a dace. At that moment, it was the most obliging, beautiful thing I could have ever hoped to see. It was as silver as the stars. It twinkled as bright as the frost, and then as I held it in my hand and the sun's last rays caught it, the scales turned to rose and flame. It was beautiful and as worthy a fish as I have ever seen and one that would be impossible to recreate if ever lost."

From In Visible Waters *John Bailey, 1984.*

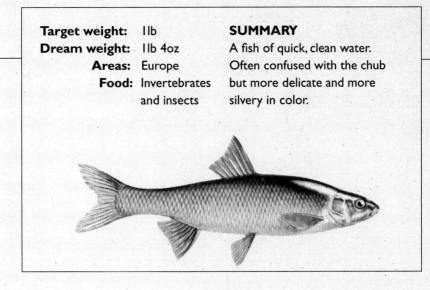

Target weight:	1lb	**SUMMARY**
Dream weight:	1lb 4oz	A fish of quick, clean water.
Areas:	Europe	Often confused with the chub
Food:	Invertebrates	but more delicate and more
	and insects	silvery in color.

It seems strange to be talking about the diminutive dace – a specimen is 10 ounces – in the company of monsters that can pull your arm out of its socket. For most of the fish in the 50, even a record dace would be a snacklet, nothing more. So many of the fish in the 50 are bruisers, dramatic, wow-look-at-me-characters with fins. The dace is none of these things. It's slim, silver and not surprisingly, an old term for it was the 'dart.'

Dace populations come and go and few people know or even care. Years ago I wrote, "It's the dace's problem that there are few men who love them and their loss is mourned only by the few. They're not large, they cannot, because of their size, put up dramatic fights. They do not taste good and so have no commercial value and because of all this, their habitat's pushed back further and further." What was true a quarter of a century ago is even more apparent now. Throughout Europe, dace habitats have become increasingly under threat and now is the time to speak up for this enchanting silver slip of a fish.

Fishing for dace is all about lightness of touch, precision, and intimacy. Because they're small, you can use the lightest of gear and because it's like gossamer, you feel every flick from the fish, every thrust of its slender body. Trotting for dace is exquisite. You need a 13 foot float rod, very fine in the tip, a center pin reel and two pound line straight through to a small hook – say a 16 or an 18. You must have a red-tipped float for the job – red somehow just goes with dace fishing. Maggots are the bait. You trickle them in at the head of a glide – dace love medium to quick paced water, some three to six feet deep and preferably over a gravel bottom.

It will probably be winter with a nip in the air because that's when dace fishing like this is at its best. The weed has gone and you can control the float perfectly, guiding it round the features that dace adore. Look for overhanging trees, for depressions in the river bed, and features of any sort. Bites are lightning. One second the float is there, riding the current and within a millisecond, it's gone. You've got to react at once. Dace can spit out a bait that feels wrong quicker than any other species on the planet. Rod bent, fish on, you won't be giving line, you won't be gasping for breath but you'll be excited when you see the fish. Its scales are so perfect, its shape supermodel

gorgeous. You will probably catch four or five fish before the shoal takes fright and scatters. Then you move on, searching water, watching the sky darken as the short winter afternoon draws to its end.

In the summer, things are rather different. You can attack dace now with the fly and this, too, is riveting stuff. Evening time is my favorite, in late June perhaps or early July. You want a warm end to the day with little wind and hopefully, there'll be hatch of flies – olives perhaps or even gnats. In fact, a Black Gnat tied on a size 20 is a difficult dry fly to beat for the dace. Some of the biggest dace in history have been caught on this method. A three-weight rod is ideal and again, the tippet shouldn't be more than two pounds, probably less. But be warned. Dace come to a dry fly quicker than any fish you will have ever seen before. If you strike before you see the fish take the fly, you will probably be just in time to hook it. You will miss, I guess, seven or eight or nine takes out of ten before you master one of the prettiest little challenges in fly fishing.

DACE FACTS

• Because dace are delicate, populations are frequently snuffed out without the world even having a clue. Dace are attacked in many low-key ways and their demise rarely makes the headlines. Years ago, at the Falls, a feeder stream was dredged in May, the most vital time for all the life that this rivulet fostered. The stream was an important spawning site which had been used for decades.

January 2008. River Wensum, England.

I'm at the Falls, probably my favourite piece of dace water in the world. There've always been big dace here. Certainly ever since I was a child. There've even been rumours of records of dace weighing an impossible one and a half pounds. A dace like this would be the equivalent of a 25 pound bonefish. It's a grey sort of day. There's drizzle that threatens to become sleet. In fact, if it weren't for the fact I'm after dace, I wouldn't be out at all. It's just that dace will give you a chance whatever the weather. It's now three in the afternoon. The light is going fast and, in truth, I've caught precious little. But there's an overflow pool here at the Falls where the water is just that little bit deeper and where I think it possible that the dace are sheltering in this cold, raw period.

I let my float wander round the pool, this way and that, hand in hand with the current. It stops. Totally unexpected this. I lift the rod tip. It jags down. A dace, a fine one. A nine ouncer, with its pigeon chest beginning to swell with spawn. I catch another half dozen fish almost all the same size, probably all shoal members since the year they were fingerlings. At the very last, with the light so gloomy I can barely see my float now, I hit into the last fish of the day. I don't weigh it. But I know it's a 12 ouncer. Twelve ounces. Not even a pound. But, there in the gloom it looms massive. You don't have to grunt and sweat to land something worthwhile. Fishing is as often about art and grace and delicacy as it is blood and guts.

BREAM *Abramis brama*

Grace and Serenity

Region: Throughout Europe and into Asia

"To many the appeal of the bream might be difficult to understand. It is not a hard-fighting fish and there are times when it swims in vast shoals and is very easy to hook and land. Indeed, small bream can be covered in slime and be as exciting as a sack of manure. A big bream, however, is something entirely different. It is difficult in the extreme to trace. It is hard to fool and there are men who have made a lifetime study of big bream and their habits."

From The Great Anglers *John Bailey, 1990.*

Target weight: 13lbs
Dream weight: 20lbs
Areas: Europe and Asia
Food: Invertebrates, insects, and occasionally small fish

SUMMARY
Bream feed mainly on invertebrates and sometimes on flies, especially midges. Big fish will also hunt small fish.

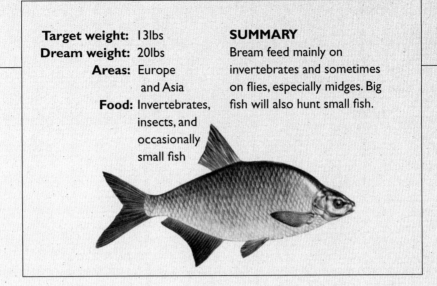

Should bream be in the 50? They're not glamorous. Top sportsmen don't pay thousands of pounds or dollars to pursue them. The bream is a fish of the common man and in a way, that's why it gets my vote. They are gentle and they are unassuming. They have a grace and a serenity that is often overlooked. They also have a wisdom that comes with age. Bream can grow old, and because they get to know their lake or pond so well, they begin to notice anything out of the ordinary and, as a result, can become very hard to catch. People who catch big bream on a regular basis do not do so by accident. A continual catcher of the species has to be dedicated and skillful and, because the biggest fish are largely nocturnal, he won't see much of his bed.

My own serious breaming years are long behind me but I remember endless, milky summer nights on some of the most beautiful waters imaginable after these lovely, cautious fish. One of the spectacular things about bream – a habit that cements their place in the 50 – is their tendency to roll on the surface, especially when they are traveling and when they're preparing to feed. A bream rolling is a wondrous sight, especially at dusk or dawn, or in the reflection of a full moon where it appears silhouetted, completely black. It's a slow, purposeful movement. For a split second, you see the head, then the back, then the erect dorsal fin, then as it disappears, a last glimpse of the tail. Sometimes bream roll and barely create a ripple. There might not be a sound. You rub your eyes, hardly able to believe that you've seen a 10 or even a 12 pound fish move so mysteriously, so secretly before you. That's what makes the bream a fish of magic. I've fished with some of the most traveled anglers in the world who haven't seen a bream roll and I always tell them they've missed one of the great events.

Of course, if you're fishing a lake at night for bream then you tend to be using two or even three rods and legering a bait on the bottom, often far out. You will lay a carpet of loose feed long before the sun goes down to attract and hold a shoal of fish wandering past. Often you will get false bites as these big-bodied fish brush against your lines. Sometimes the bites will be very tentative, a bobbin just rising or falling an inch. It's all very tense, tingling with excitement. When eventually the bobbin

rises and holds there and you sweep the rod back and feel the pressure of a hooked fish...well, believe me, it's a moment you're glad you're bream fishing.

But bream aren't always fish of the darkness and of stillwaters. Nowadays, on the Hampshire Avon in England, they live in some of the quickest, clearest, shallowest of reaches. You can catch them trotting a worm down under a float or rolling a piece of sweetcorn along the bottom. You can actually see these great fish – some of them weigh towards double figures – coming in, tipping up and browsing over the bait. There will be puffs of silt escaping, drifting off downstream, alerting other fish that there is food on the table. Soon, you might have 10 or even 15 bream grubbing in front of you. When you hook one, they roll, showing their immense depth and their wondrous, mahogany coloring.

BREAM FACTS

• Because they're common, they are at low risk. But because they're large it doesn't mean to say that they're not very sensitive. It's been traditional to keep large catches of bream in keep nets for the big trophy shot at the end of the session. Remember, please, that bream hemorrhage badly if held in confinement like this. Their protective slime is removed and their scales can be levered back. The stress this can cause can result in serious and long term damage.

February 1976. From John Bailey's Fishing Diary.

Fishing the Big Bend as usual. Got here at around dusk and fished until 7:45am when I have the first bite. The bobbin just lurched crazily towards the butt. A good fight. A big fish wallowing. And guess what, a bream. Six and a half pounds. What is noticeable about it is a big black spot on the tail root. A cracking fish. Of course, I'm constantly hoping for roach but a river bream is always good. See the fox again working around the farm buildings on my way off the flood plain. A big dog he is. Will try to photograph him one dusk now I know his movements.

November 1987. From John Bailey's Fishing Diary.

Wow. How about this? I'm fishing down at the Big Bend again after a gap of perhaps 10 years. I love the place still. It's lovely to be nestled in the reeds again after such a long time. And you won't guess this. I left a rod rest the last time I fished a decade ago. And it's still there tonight, battered, bent, rusted but unmistakably mine. And there's more. What's also unmistakably mine is the bream I caught. Yes, it's got a spot on its tail. He's a friend I remember from 11 years back. This time I weighed him in at just over nine pounds so he's put on three pounds in weight during that period. He still looks fantastic. Deeper bodied now. Brilliant condition. An exciting fish all round. Once again, he's happy with bread as bait and once again I catch him well into darkness.

July 2002. From John Bailey's Fishing Diary.

Blimey! The Big Bend. Arrive about two in the afternoon. The water is crystal and I pick up a reasonable roach first cast. I look down at my feet. There's a ledge about six feet deep before dropping off to some 11 or 12. On the ledge there's a fish feeding, a really big bream. I let a bait fall down about two or three feet ahead of it and I watch. The bream's in no hurry. He looks completely serene, completely at ease as he approaches the bait, a single grain of corn on a size 14 hook. When he sees it, he accelerates and up-ends over it. A huge shield of light as he reflects the sun. I hold my strike for a couple of seconds to make sure the bait's passed the lips and when I strike, he rolls drunkenly before heading off with real purpose into deep water. It's a great fight. This is a great fish and in the sunlight he looks even more imposing. I get him in and I recognize him at once. Black spot. Twenty-six years on and still alive and happy and more than double the weight that he was when I first landed him. Terrific coloring. I'm so excited to catch him again I slide him back without a proper weight or a photograph. A shame perhaps but I don't want to stress him out ever again... so closely have our lives mirrored each other.

PERCH *Perca fluviatilis*

Striped Hunter

Region: Europe and Asia

"Our guide told us over dinner that perch of two pound are no problem. Four pounds, he said, wobbling his head, a bit of a problem. Six pounds? Bigger problem. Eight pounds? He shrugged his shoulders. Yes, they're a problem he admits. But we try. This is a perch paradise."

From John Bailey's fishing diary, Ukraine, 1995.

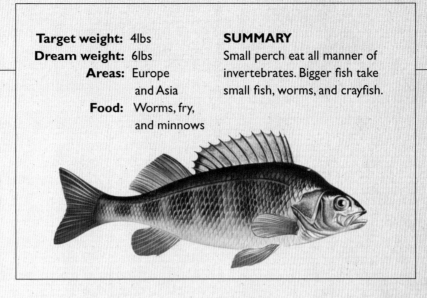

Target weight: 4lbs
Dream weight: 6lbs
Areas: Europe and Asia
Food: Worms, fry, and minnows

SUMMARY
Small perch eat all manner of invertebrates. Bigger fish take small fish, worms, and crayfish.

There's a bit of nostalgia going on here. Perch, in part, make the 50 because of a day nearly half a century ago when I caught my first 'proper' fish on rod and line. And it was a perch. A fine, bristling two ouncer patrolling the margins of the canal. It saw my worm. Its dorsal fin shot erect, its pectorals quivering. It came up to the worm. It huffed and it puffed and it sucked it down. I struck so hard the fish catapulted from the water, disappeared over my left shoulder and buried itself in a hedge. But I found it. I revered it. And I let it go. What a wonderful, wonderful fish.

Perch and those broad bands of theirs make them look like American football players. That's in their character, too.

They hunt in packs. They swagger. They chase anything smaller than themselves. Those spined, look-at-me dorsal fins show attitude. No, you don't mess with a perch. Otters do, though. I've just lost one of my best ever perch pools to them. It's only a couple of acres but for three years I've been enjoying some of the best perch fishing of my life. First they were two pounders. Then three pounders. Then they were heading on towards four when the otters found them. We've been finding perch on the banks like dustbin lids with just a chunk taken out – generally round the shoulders or out of the belly. I could weep. Really. That's the thing with perch: they come and they go like no other species. If you find a perch water, then I suggest you fish it, enjoy it and remember it with affection because it won't last forever.

of bigger than that! This guy, too, was drunk but this time he swore he'd seen these perch himself. Four fish weighing a total of 60 pounds. You can work that one out for yourself!

Interestingly, these monsters were reputed to have come from the brackish waters of the Black Sea. Now, obviously, I can't say whether they ever existed or not but I can agree that perch like a dash of salt. For example, you can catch them round the harbors and the islands of Copenhagen. It's surreal, sitting outside at a bar, amidst all the traffic, looking down into the crystal water and watching three and four and five pound perch mooching amongst the anchor chains of ships. I've seen a huge perch, too, come out of the Baltic Sea along the Swedish coastline. The fish was taken a mile or more from the shore and when I laid it on the boards of the boat, crabs scuttled out of the weed that it rested upon. As I picked it up to slide it back, I felt its stomach crunch and grind under my fingers. It was upon crabs that the perch had obviously been feeding.

Another reason perch are in the 50 is because they're unexpected. You never quite know with perch. Jim, a close neighbor of mine, has a wonderful garden pool. It was full of tiny, stunted goldfish so, one day, he brought a couple of perch from one of his farm ponds and put them in. They were about a pound and he reckoned they'd do well. Then he forgot all about them. Some years later, a well-known salmon angler was staying with him. They decided to try out a new rod and after plenty of brandy went onto the veranda to flick a tube fly over the pool. First pull back it was taken. Wham. Bang. A perch of four and a half pounds. A fish of a lifetime.

The question is, just how big do perch grow? This isn't always important with a lot of fish species, but it is with perch. The reason is that I just have a feeling that there might be much, much bigger perch about on the planet than we actually know of. Remember my guide and his four kilo fish? Four kilos – in old money is edging towards 10 pounds. Blooming enormous. But I've even heard of bigger. All right, the man was drunk and he admitted he hadn't seen them himself but I met up with a Czech geologist who swore that somewhere in Turkey he'd heard of a 12 pounder! And I've even heard

PERCH FACTS

• Perch range throughout the UK, across northern Europe and well into Asia. Risks to the species are low but it's as well to remember that they grow fast and live for a comparatively short time.

• One of the delights of perch fishing is that they can be caught on fly, lure, or bait. Perhaps the best fun of all is to fish for them with a variety of small, plastic jigs. Small fish and worm patterns are favorite.

August 1966. Cley sluice gates, Norfolk, England.

It's the summer holidays and the six of us spend all our time on our push bikes cycling from one pond to the next. It's glorious. We've had tench, rudd, roach, eels, trout, dace, crucian carp and today we're going to catch some perch. We've seen them by the sluice gates, right at the bottom of the River Glaven where it runs through the salt marsh and out to the sea. Of course the place is tidal there's a rise and fall of at least three feet on even a small tide. And this is what we've begun to realize. The perch actually like it when the tide's in and the water's more salt than sweet. We realize that they're hunting sand eels, small flatties, smelts, crabs and everything else that the salt brings with it.

We can see the perch hunting just beneath the road bridge, the seaward side of the sluice gates. There are lots of them and they're big. Where they go when the tide's low we don't know, we don't care; our plan is built around the high water. We've got some sticklebacks in a pail. Not long ago they were our target fish and now they're just our bait. We've grown up. We'll fish them under a float, letting them bob along with the tide, working them in and out along the banks of reeds.

We're spread out all the way down as far as the windmill and Mike gets the first. It's big and we all pile down to see it. What a mighty fish it is lying there in the wet grasses. Our eyes widen with jealousy and we run back to our rods.

I get mine half an hour later at the height of the tide. The float plummets. The fish fights in a jagged, heavy, sullen sort of way. I'm screaming for help and Bill, this time, arrives with an old net. We weigh it on my scales and then on his. There's four ounce discrepancy so it either weighs two pounds 11 ounces (his scales) or two pounds 15 ounces (my scales). I decide on the latter. Bill suggests we check the scales but I'm not having that.

The fish is in my bag, across my shoulder, being pedalled home for my grandmother to cook. That's what old folk do. They'll eat just about anything. Even my biggest ever perch.

SPANISH BARBEL

Barbus comizo (and other.

Fish as Bright as Canaries

Region: Spain and Portugal

"Gypsy barbel," my old friend in the bar said to me. 'That's what we call them, in private. Andalucian barbel is better for you, my friend, though. Remember that. A point importante. These are the most beautiful fish in the world and the ones no-one knows."

From John Bailey's fishing diary, June 1999.

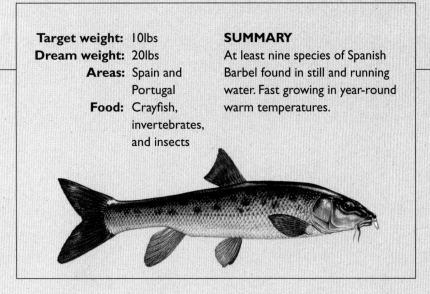

Target weight: 10lbs
Dream weight: 20lbs
Areas: Spain and Portugal
Food: Crayfish, invertebrates, and insects

SUMMARY
At least nine species of Spanish Barbel found in still and running water. Fast growing in year-round warm temperatures.

Let's deal with the biology. The room in which this book is being written is lined by my fishing library. I've been collecting fishing books now since the 1950s and I have them in their thousands. I have a pile of 23 books on the biology of fish around the world. There's not a single one that mentions anything in depth about the species of barbel to be found in Spain. One book vaguely covers the comizo and says they peter out at around seven or eight pounds – Comizos grow to 40 pounds. There's a mention of the Boca barbel, indicating they may weigh four or five pounds. I once photographed one that weighed 20. Of Andalucian barbel, there isn't a mention. This is, of course, exciting because it's like these fish are totally off the academic map. It's like these fish belong to us, the anglers alone. And that, to me, lends the fish a huge and special enchantment.

threading it through the tail and I swung it out into the middle of the shoal. They scattered. An hour later I relocated them. This time, I put the crayfish well on the far side of them and twitched it, slowly back into the group. One of the biggest fish, 25 pounds plus, peeled off and followed the cray down five feet to the bottom of the crystal clear stream. It looked at it a full minute... you could see the question marks. And then, it moved off with its fellows upstream and I lost them for the rest of the day. And that's as close as I've been to a mammoth comizo. I've fared better, much better with Andalucians.

Let's deal with comizos first. On a few occasions I've fished from a bridge in a town in Extremadura, into a river that is paved with comizos. I've caught scores up to around 10 pounds but never contacted the monsters. But one day, I so nearly did. About 30 miles upstream of this particular town the river in question breaks into a number of threads, all deep, clear and narrow. Here, I located a group of about 20 comizos moving rapidly along a beat about half a mile long. The fish were obviously spooky, aware of my presence, and they were very, very large. The smallest fish I estimated at 20 pounds and the largest could not have been far short of 30. They were an impressive sight in the boiling sunshine as they bow waved in the water course.

I laid out several beds of bait hoping to pull them down and to get them feeding. After several hours, this tactic proved to be totally in vain. I knew that comizos are intensely predatorial and I, therefore, set to work turning over large rocks in the margins of the stream. Soon I had four large, aggressive signal crayfish in my tiny bucket. I was ready for a more radical approach.

Again, I stalked the water, this time very slowly, keeping myself well hidden. After some 20 minutes I located a group of fish circling slowly around under some eucalyptus trees. I put on a medium-sized crayfish,

SPANISH BARBEL FACTS

• Fly fishing for barbel is a welcome bonus. A six-weight outfit with floating line is generally suitable. Target Andalucian barbel feeding in the surface film with small black and brown flies. Black gnats, Adams, Blue-winged Olives, and most CDC patterns work well. Size 14 Pheasant Tail nymphs are excellent for fish working in the deeper pools. Most of the barbel average between two and six pounds and this gear is adequate for all but the occasional monster.

September 2005. Walking Mr. Henderson's Railway, Andalucia, Spain.

You leave the village and come directly to the railway and the river both. The rail track twists and turns down the valley never more than 20 yards from the water for seven miles to the next scattering of houses. This is Mr. Henderson's railway. Way back in the 19th century this British railway engineer was charged with building a line from Granada in the north to Algeciras in the south and I'm glad that he did. Without him the most perfect day any angler could imagine would not exist.

It's nine in the morning. The sun is hot and beneath you, the Andalucian river is heaving with barbel sipping in flies. You've got a fly rod with you. A six-weight. Floating line. Six pound leader. A box of nymphs and a box of dry flies from mayflies down to the tiniest of black gnats.

Now, you're turning right passing an old, deserted farmhouse with palms in the yard and you're heading up the crag. The whole valley unwinds beneath you, the railway track to the right of the river.

It's indescribably beautiful. The vegetation even in June is still lush and green. Flowers dazzle everywhere and the footpath beckons you, leading you to over a score of pools unfished since your last visit. Old Man's Garden. Old Farmhouse Pool. The Hole in the Wall. The Wooden Bridge Run. Al's Corner. The Beach. Goat Trail. Tunnel Bend. Otter Pool. Coi Corner. (Don't ask.) Jungle Run. Tumbledown Pool. All enchanting, all challenging, all full of barbel.

Old Man's Garden is in the shadow of the railway itself, quick at the neck and at the tail but slow and deep in the belly. A mayfly patterns trick two fish into rising and you hook the second that sets off like a Pamplona bull that's seen red. You're upriver and downriver after it and, a full 10 minutes later, you can't believe it weighs four pounds. The morning carries on blissfully. You fish and you walk. You walk and you fish. Trains rumble past. You see faces pressed against the windows. A goatherd drives his animals through the valley and your Spanish is just good enough for a chat about the biggest fish that he's ever seen in the river. He points to a hole in the cliff face. "Look. Look," he says and you see the face of an Egyptian mongoose staring at you wide-eyed and suspicious.

It's approaching the mid-afternoon when you pull into the downstream village and walk through the outskirts where the dogs bark and the chickens peck the dirt. Have you had 15 fish? Was it 20? Who cares? You remember the biggest at seven pounds. Brilliant. The Quercus Restaurant is the place to eat here. The woman there is olive-skinned, brown hair, lustrous eyes and she smiles at you. Olives on the table outside. Ice cold beer. You look through the flies in your box. Adams were the best. Size 16. A big black nymph tied on a 12 accounted for three fish, though, you remember. Two flies are bent out of all recognition. That second fish was a monster.

One course drifts into the next. The heat of the afternoon begins to fade. The Rioja takes its effect and it's with a jolt that you realize it's eight minutes to six, a bill has to be paid, and a train has to be caught. As you rattle up the valley, you sit on the right hand of the train so you can watch the course of the river where you've just been fishing. Each pool is instantly recognizable and each one has its tale of disasters and successes. Back at your own village, the station bar is busy with old men playing dominoes. Another beer is called for as you watch them laugh and play. The sky is darkening and the stars are beginning to appear.

BURBOT *Lota lota*

The Mysterious Freshwater Cod

Region: North America, Europe, and Siberia

"The status of some rare fish species in Britain, for example, Aliss shad, Twaite shad, Arctic char, the White fishes, smelt, sturgeon, and burbot are poorly known and urgently need further study before they disappear for good. In the case of burbot, this may already have happened."

Freshwater Fish of the British Isles *Nick Giles, 1994.*

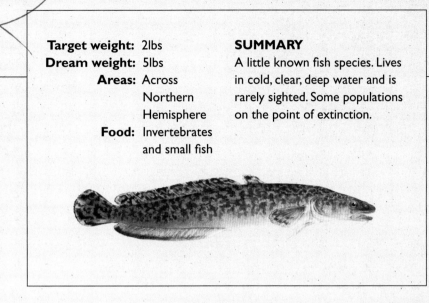

Target weight: 2lbs
Dream weight: 5lbs
Areas: Across Northern Hemisphere
Food: Invertebrates and small fish

SUMMARY
A little known fish species. Lives in cold, clear, deep water and is rarely sighted. Some populations on the point of extinction.

Once upon a time, in England, the burbot, or the eel pout, was a common and ill-respected creature. In fact, go back to the Middle Ages, they were, apparently, so abundant that they were netted out of Fenland water courses and fed in vast quantities to the pigs as an easy source of rich protein. When I was a kid, the old Norfolk boys remembered catching burbot with ease in the rivers to the extreme west of the county. It seems they caught them on worm at night when they were after eels. Nobody regarded them much it seems.

They were just there, rather like toads or worms or bats or moles…just a low-key part of England's flora and fauna, not much thought about.

And then, suddenly, the world wakes up to realize that burbot aren't about anymore. I guess it was sometime in the 1950s or 1960s that somebody said to his fishing companion, "Haven't caught any burbot lately, have we?" Then, the question began to be asked nationwide. By the 1960s, a hunt was on for the burbot.

Opinions differ as to when the last burbot was taken from a British waterway. Some say it was the Sixties. Others uphold that a burbot was caught from the Great Ouse system 30 years back. It was this glorious uncertainty, that made me, in the 1990s, pursue burbot for a short time with absolute intensity.

It was the River Thet in the south of the county where rumors of most burbot were last to be seen and it was there that I fished. As my old boys indicated, I tended to fish worm and small dead minnows at night, rather like I would for eels. And eels were what I landed. Every time the line shot out, my heart would leap. Playing a fish in the darkness, you never quite knew, not until the torch was shone. Then, sadly, I would record another eel. I covered a lot of water. I fished a lot of nights. I asked a lot of questions of a lot of people. But burbot and Bailey, it seemed, were never destined to meet. A day in 1994 changed all that.

In those days, I'd go on any fishing trip, anywhere in the world no matter how hair-brained, how ill-conceived. In the August of this particular year, I travelled with a group of Germans far, far east into Siberia. Everything about the trip was a disaster. The travel. The guiding.

The camp. Food supplies. Even the fishing. The rivers had been pretty well raped by local fishermen and an absence of supplies forced us to fish desperately and quite literally for our lives. For a 10 day period, we all existed primarily on a diet of sardine-sized Siberian grayling. Catching them, too, was no fun. As soon as temperatures began to rise from the bone-crunching coldness of the night, the mosquitoes appeared in appalling numbers. There was nothing, nothing good about this trip until…

BURBOT FACTS

• Burbot need cold water. They like water temperatures below 45°F (7°C) and they feed best in the winter, retreating to the coldest depths in the summer. Perhaps that's where I got it wrong on the Thet. Perhaps I shouldn't have fished the summer but the coldest of winter nights. Though I doubt if it would have done me actually any good at all.

August, 1994. Siberia.

What a night it was. It was cold. Thank God. Total bliss. Not a mosquito in the air. We sat in the black crispness, keeping the campfire roaring. George cooked one of my lenok a la carte, with onions, tomatoes and doused in some of the last of our champagne. We drank. We sang badly but we were at last happy, quite content to grab a few minutes of calm.

Six a.m. I'm called by the hunter to check his nets. It's a blissful clear morning with a crisp blanket of frost. We walk the bank to check the first two nets. There are bear prints on the beach and the hunter is worried the animal might have destroyed the nets. We find a small lenok and a grayling. A start, at least, for tonight's supper. My tummy bug hits me happily minutes before the first real wave of mosquitoes. Every cloud has its silver lining. Now we cross the river in the rubber inflatable and it's the usual, terrifying journey. Nets three and four lie in a backwater, five or six feet deep with a slight current running through. Net three another lenok. Net four a BURBOT!!!!! Though physically I want to die, mentally I'm hopping with excitement!!!

The hunter can't believe my excitement. The creature lies in a puddle of water and I'm almost too excited to take a photograph. I focus on it. In truth, he's an ugly little critter with his mottled, cowpat-colored skin, his wicked little goatee beard, his bulbous eyes and his roly-poly sausage roll body. But no matter, I have my burbot picture at last.

I half think to plead with the hunter for the fish's life but that would be mad given our present predicament. Back at the camp where everybody else still sleeps, the burbot is cooked by simply leaning it against a cooking pot. Growling, gurgling stomach or not, it must be tried. It's got a cod-like texture. It's very salty and that's not just the cook's doing at all. I chew my first forkful and it's not remotely swallowable. It goes from fish to a kind of wood pulp and then to a sort of grainy chewing gum. I don't like to say this but I suppose you see why it is hard for the Great British public to lament the loss of the burbot too keenly. In fact, after meeting him, even I haven't a great desire to renew the acquaintance.

MAHSEER *Barbus tor*

The Jewel of the Crown

Region: Himalayan kingdoms, north and south India, Sri Lanka

"The thrill of a big mahseer hooked in heavy water, hurtling himself down the rapids with express speed to the tune of a fast emptying reel, has an electric joy which sets it apart from any other sport. Once experienced, it's imprinted on the tablets of memory. Many a sportsman would say he would rather catch a big mahseer than shoot a tiger."

From John Bailey's diary

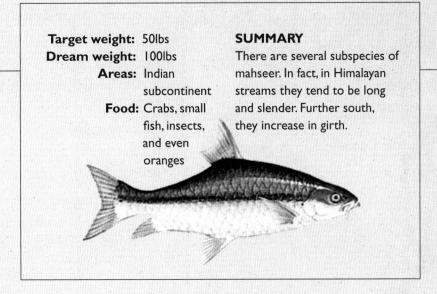

Target weight: 50lbs
Dream weight: 100lbs
Areas: Indian subcontinent
Food: Crabs, small fish, insects, and even oranges

SUMMARY
There are several subspecies of mahseer. In fact, in Himalayan streams they tend to be long and slender. Further south, they increase in girth.

Without doubt, the mahseer is the hardest fighting fish in freshwater. You can admire the cunning of the mahseer because these are old and educated fish. You can gawp at the beauty of the mahseer because in their differing shades of gold, silver and black, these are fabulous creatures. But it is the sheer force and brutality of the mahseer's first run that makes the species cruise into the 50 list. You can stop a mahseer sometimes.

Perhaps. You will lose pieces of finger as you jam down on the flying spool. Blood will flow but even so, mostly the mahseer will get the better of you. If a 50 pounder begins to run, expect a hundred even 200 yards of line to disappear in seconds. A 100 pounder will take you to the knot on the spool. Phenomenal force is what mahseer fishing is all about.

If you're mahseer fishing in north India along the Ganges or the Brahmaputra tributaries or in Nepal, a 20 pound fish is good and a 40 pounder is great. Down south, along the Cauvery in Karnataka, be proud of a 40 and simply worship anything over 70 or even 80 pounds. Above 90 pounds, these fish are like battleships, armour-plated, muscles of steel.

Mahseer aren't as rare as tiger yet but if you're brave and interested in pitching yourself against the most ferocious fish of freshwater, don't delay the experience. Northern fish are threatened by deforestation, southern fish by the giddying growth of cities, Bangalore in particular, and the resulting water abstraction. The Cauvery river, especially, is gravely threatened. Unless mahseer are recognized and protected, the big fish of history will, in truth, be creatures of the past.

There are mysteries in this river of dreams, the Cauvery. Ninety pounders and low 100 pounders are the monsters of hard fact. The guides, though, insist fish of 150 pounds, even 200 pounds are present, grown old, wary and virtually uncatchable. Even if hooked, could such a fish ever be landed? Years ago, in one of the upper camps, an American woman hooked just such a fish. She fought it for three hours. The fish was seen many times. A 130, even 150 pounder was the estimate. Then it was like the fish awoke and it ran irresistibly, eternally. The spool emptied and the line broke as if a pistol had just been shot.

MAHSEER FACTS

• The mahseer is one of the largest members of the world carp family. In the north of India and the countries along the Himalayas, it is a longer, slimmer fish than you find in the south. Here, the fish are broader, deeper and come in strains of gold, silver and, less frequently, black.

• Fishing in the north is generally all about spinning with plugs or big silver spoons. Spinning does take place in the south but most of the fishing is done with ragi paste.

January, 2008 Cauvery River, South India.

Alberto Gonzalez is more fortunate. The fishing has been quiet for days. The dam upriver is holding back water for Bangalore taps and the rapids are too shallow for the big fish which are forced to drop back into the huge pool known as Crocodile Rock. Croc is full of fish but it's half a mile long, up to 80 feet deep and, in places, is 100 yards across so location is a problem. In the almost static water, the fish also have an age to inspect any bait. You can actually feel lumps of ragi paste the size of a tennis ball being picked up, tested and oh-so-gently being replaced gently on the river bed. These are big fish as aware of our presence as we are of theirs. It's spooky and frustrating stuff.

As a result, this blisteringly hot afternoon, Alberto and his guide take their coracle to the tail of Croc Rock where the water speeds up and begins to empty into a set of rapids. Alberto is hoping big fish will be there looking for increased oxygen, perhaps hunting for small fish and freshwater crabs. It's his first cast, a little after 10 past four and the ball of ragi paste is taken ferociously. The fight is mad, furious, back-wrenching, painful in the heat. But it's over quickly. After a 'mere' 45 minutes, a vast golden mahseer is tethered on a stringer, being ferried to shallower, more friendly water. One of the great ceremonies of freshwater fishing is about to begin.

The weighing and photographing of a massive mahseer burns itself into your memory forever. First, there's the exhaustion and the bewildered exaltation of the angler. Alberto looks dazed, can barely speak, he's close to tears of the purest, most ecstatic joy. But then you see the fish, wallowing at the end of the stringer. The sun picks out its scales and then flashes on the dorsal fin as it breaks the surface of the river. That dorsal fin is impossibly massive. It represents the pride and the power of these mythical fish.

TIGER FISH

Hydrocynus forskalii

The Fiercest Fish

Region: Africa

"I have stated heretofore in print and I'm still ready to maintain my pronouncement, that the tiger fish of Africa is the fiercest fish that swims. Let others hold forth as advocates for the Mako shark, the barracuda, the piranha of the Amazon, or the blue fish of the Atlantic. To them I say tish and tush! This sweeping challenge is not issued on behalf of the mighty Goliath tiger fish – to whom I bow, hat in hand – but is offered in tribute to the common or garden poor relation tiger fish that abound throughout northern and tropical Africa. Small though they may be, they're quite fierce enough and tough enough to earn my deepest respect and admiration."

Leander J. McCormick Game Fish of the World 1949.

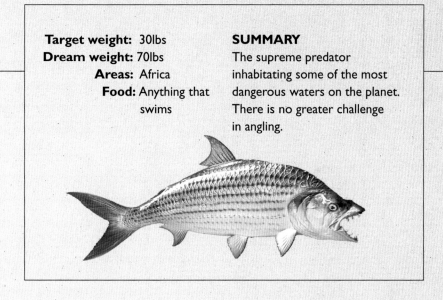

Target weight: 30lbs	**SUMMARY**
Dream weight: 70lbs	The supreme predator
Areas: Africa	inhabiting some of the most
Food: Anything that swims	dangerous waters on the planet. There is no greater challenge in angling.

SUMMARY

The supreme predator inhabiting some of the most dangerous waters on the planet. There is no greater challenge in angling.

There are four or five species of tiger fish but let's concentrate on two. McCormick's common or garden tiger fish and the Goliath. The former grows to perhaps 20 to 30 pounds, and, in the case of Goliath, the sky is the potential limit. A 100 pounder certainly is possible, perhaps 200 but let's not speculate.

I'll come clean at once and say my own tiger fish credentials are non-existent. I've had a few small ones from the shores of lakes possibly up to five pounds in weight and they've scared me to death. I've found them beautiful to look at, terrifyingly pugnacious, very difficult to hook, and even more difficult to unhook. The teeth of even a five pound tiger fish are ghastly. It's a fish well named. So, does the 'normal' tiger fish deserve to get into the 50? Perhaps not quite – it's a real honor to get near it after all. But the Goliath. That's a different matter altogether. If you ask me honestly, I'll tell you this: the Goliath tiger fish is very probably the most significant notch any on-the-edge angler can hope to hew on his belt. The Goliath is rare. The Goliath is difficult to locate. The Goliath is difficult to hook, even though its attack on a lure or a bait is violence itself. The Goliath fights like a rabid dog enraged. The Goliath lives in some of the most naturally threatening waters in the world. Whoever has caught a Goliath and lived deserves our respect.

Our friend McCormick quotes the Goliath expert of the early 20th century, the redoubtable Doctor Gillet who resided for over 30 years in what was then the Belgian Congo. He was the medical inspector there and, during his leisure time pursued the Goliath in many areas of the Congo River system. Let's have a look at what the madcap Gillet has to say…

"The teeth in a specimen of 40 or 50 pounds may be two inches long and nearly four tenths of an inch wide at the base…the shameful truth is that Goliaths are superbly cannibalistic. The best bait for Goliath is a smaller Goliath. It is a matter of water dog eat water dog. This River Congo must be no place for an animal with a weak heart. The four important cohabitants are crocodiles, Nile perch and the two varieties of tiger fish. Each of these is possessed of an insatiable craving to devour their own kind as well as the others…tiger fish gobble up young crocodiles with the greatest zest and crocodiles certainly return the compliment. The Nile perch helps itself to both and is itself the victim of the others. Thus we have a perfect example of a mutual devouration society – the state of affairs which probably accounts for the comparatively small number of Goliaths that reach full maturity…among the natives,

Goliath is regarded as a doubtful asset. They claim it attacks them when swimming and shows a predilection for biting off their genitals…if there is a cataract, a waterfall or otherwise unnavigable section of river available, one can be sure that tiger fish will congregate there. Failing these water hazards, it will choose for its home those parts of the rivers that flow through impenetrable jungles, teeming with poisonous snakes, leopards, buffalos, and elephants. Of course, such places will also swarm with tsetse flies and malarial mosquitoes…the life of a tiger fish seems incomplete without the hippopotamus and the crocodile… for some reason, hippos cannot resist capsizing small boats. Possibly they mean no harm, but then you may find yourself struggling in water stiff with crocodiles. You have always been told that crocodiles are cowardly creatures but in such circumstances you are apt to be sceptical. You figure that if a crocodile bites you in half, the tiger fish will grab off anything that is left over."

Hmm. When it comes to Goliaths, I'm, at my age, a fully paid up member of the cowards' club. I'm not proud about this but I'm not beating myself up unduly. In 25 years of almost ceaseless travelling I've been in an air crash, charged by a tigress, been shot at, been imprisoned in a jungle jail, contracted malaria, been pursued by a snake, been drained by the most virulent viruses on the planet, and have even had a leopard try to get into bed with me. I'm not at all sure that even a certain promise of a 100 pound Goliath would get me on the Congo today. But it wasn't long ago that it nearly did.

TIGER FISH FACTS

• It would be stupid for me to speculate about anything regarding Goliath tiger fish. All I can say is that in my library collected life long, I have two books that you ought to consult if you're mad enough to be interested. The first is *The Largest Tiger Fish in the World – The Goliath* by Douglas Dann. The second book is one of the classics of the 20th century – *Somewhere Down the Crazy River* by Paul Boote and Jeremy Wade (Sangha Books 1992).

"John, you can't begin to understand how lucky you were not to make this trip with us. I know you were fearing the worst, terrified that you would have missed out on the trip of your lifetime. It's as well you had to go to Russia. You missed an adventure from hell. Where do I begin?

"The flight into this desperate lawless capital? The dreadful nights spent in the most stinking hotel? The journey up the Congo in boats that can be described as little more than death traps? The lack of food? The putrid water? The surly guides? The continually biting insects? The threat of soldiers, day and night, checking our papers, taking our goods? The complete lack of fishing? Never once did we wet a line. Never once did we see a sign of Goliath.

"The boats broke down. We were late back. We missed our flight. We had to spend a further week at the mercy of our murderous, corrupt guides. We were all lucky to escape with our lives. I exaggerate not a word. If anyone ever mentions Goliath to you again, put your hands over your ears and scream till they leave you. You say Russia wasn't easy. You were on a picnic compared to us."

AMUR PIKE

Esox reichertii

Leopard Patterned Pike of Legend

Region: Asia – broadly the catchment area of Amur River

"I'm beginning to feel as though this is a wild goose chase. Every Mongolian I meet tells me there are Amur Pike to be had here in the system that I'm fishing. But you know that they want to oblige, that they're aware this is what I want to hear. Time might tell. Or it might not."

From John Bailey's Mongolian diary, 24th September 1998.

Target weight: 20lbs
Dream weight: 40lbs
Areas: Far East Asia
and China
Food: Fish

SUMMARY
Esox reichertii – exactly like
Esox lucius (northern pike)
in habitat and diet. Only by a
freak of nature of the east/west
divide, their skin patterns are
exactly reversed.

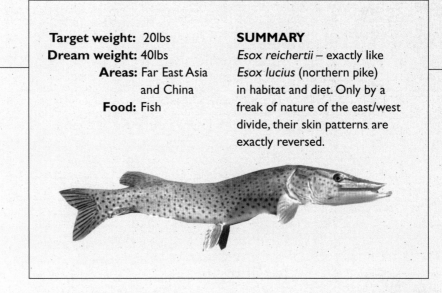

The Amur pike gets into the 50 on the simple fact of its rarity. I'm not aware of any 'easy' way to an Amur pike. My suspicion is that anyone who wants to catch one of these fabled creatures will have to do it the hard way. Like we did. If you like your fishing extreme, then it could be an expedition after Amurs is for you.

I state from the outset that I have no clear idea as to the boundaries of Amur pike territory. Sense dictates that these are fish found in the catchment area of the vast Amur system that dominates a huge swathe of Far East Asia.

Whether the entire system holds Amurs or parts of it, I have no way of telling you. There is information to be found but, like a lot of what comes from these areas, exact, verifiable detail is often thin on the ground.

I tackled Amurs in Far East Mongolia, close to the Chinese border. To say this is a wild, desolate area is a gross understatement. There are occasional townships, ugly places, sad reminders of those times when the government tried to force this nomadic people into bleak, communist-style communities.

Once outside these decaying urban sprawls, there are millions of acres of absolute nothingness. This is the area of the Onon River and its plains upon which roam wild horses, great bustards, and wolves aplenty. Here and there are rough tracks and you might come across the odd broken down, rusted Jeep but that's about all you will see. Rivers are still crossed by ferries and you might have to wait a day or more for the ferryman. This isn't a place which you get around in easily.

In fact, when leaving it, my group and I nearly lost our lives. We had clambered aboard a 46-year-old Antonov An-2 to take us back to Ulan Bataar. A couple of hours into the journey, the engine faltered and gave out and it was only the consummate skill of the Mongolian pilot that effected a successful crash landing. And we in the West complain of an occasional late train!

The majority of the group were principally after taimen. The species in the east of Mongolia flaunts a scarlet red tail as opposed to the orange ones further to the west. In our pursuit we had had reasonable success. But I hankered more and more strongly after an Amur. Then on September 25th, Ennisch, our guide, told us that he had heard of a lagoon off the arm of the Onon some seven or eight miles from our camp. We would have to walk.

Temperatures that day reached 95°F (35°C) and the trek was up cliffs, down gorges and through bogs. Those seven miles took four hours to accomplish. But, indeed, the place looked tantalizing. The river had flooded an area of flat land some 25 or 30 acres in extent and shoals of small silver fish could be seen dimpling the surface. Hopes understandably ran high. Still, it was mid-afternoon before the Professor began to call wildly from the far bank. We got round to him as he was preparing to lift a small pike from the water. From our vantage point on the bank, the pike looked absolutely no different to our own *esox lucius*. Fortunately, once lifted into the sun we all gasped. Though the fish was lean and probably weighed no more than five pounds, it was a beauty. Though in profile the fish was totally pike, its markings were outrageous. Those mahogany spots on a creamy-white background were simply impossible to take in fully. I, particularly, was exultant. The trek back to our camp seemed more like a magic carpet.

AMUR PIKE FACTS

• My own feeling is that Amur pike are similar to *esox lucius* in virtually every way apart from their coloring. This would lead me to believe that normal pike methods are the ones to adopt. All I would add is that this is a very difficult part of the world to exist in safely. Do your homework carefully if planning a trip. Remember, in this part of the world, there are guides that often don't offer the level of service that we have grown used to expecting in the West.

September 1996. The Onon Junction, East Mongolia.

My own chance came a week or so later. Once again, Ennisch had decided on a plan. Together we took an ancient iron-clad boat through the marshes to a spot where the Onon met one of its more serious tributaries. Here, as Ennisch had predicted, there was a big, deep, fishy-looking pool. I was spinning with large silver spoons and, at first, all I could catch were taimen. I had three good ones, perhaps to 25 pounds when I hooked into a fish that was completely different. It fought much more deeply with strong but shorter runs. It was evidently a big fish.

Now Ennisch and I are truly excited. We haven't seen the fish for five minutes, a long time when you're using a rod of immense power and 30 pound line. The sun's high. The water's clear. The fish, despite my efforts, remains glued to the bottom. Every now and again showers of bubbles hit the surface and I'm beginning to fear that I could have hooked into a catfish.

There's no doubt now. The fish is coming up. We're both straining to see what we're hooked into, leaning precariously over the side of the tin-pot boat. I think I see it first. My Polaroids are probably of superior quality. It's a pike. It's an Amur. It's seriously big. The fish comes closer and closer to the surface. Ennisch is beginning to set up the net. I tell him it's too soon and I'm right. In a great vortex of water and with an angry slap of a huge tail, the pike is gone, the spoon is dangling in the air and we're both devastated. We fish on and on throughout the day, trying all the coves and creeks in the area but all we catch is a couple more taimen and large, beautifully spoofed Onon trout. But, back in camp, we decide to rate this a success. Though the fish hasn't been landed, the presence of big Amurs we have at least confirmed.

PIKE *Esox lucius*

The Water Wolf of Legend
Region: North America, Europe, and Siberia

Pike. Its very name fires the mind, evoking pictures of half forgotten things: wind-blown leaves of autumn, slanting to dark reedy meres where log-like monsters with marble eyes hang motionless on faintly quivering fins...before a sudden slash send shoals of prey-fish scattering in confusion through the mist. What other fish so grips the imagination, filling it with terror, repugnance, wonder, awe?

Hugh Falkus

Target weight:	25lbs
Dream weight:	40lbs
Areas:	USA, Europe, and Asia
Food:	Fish

SUMMARY
Determined carnivores, pikes feed on other fish, particularly roach, as well as insects and amphibians.

We are only interested in large pike here, monsters even. A monstrous pike – say over 30 pounds – will be a female. All the monsters are. This great she-fish will not be the water wolf of legend, some embodiment of piscine evil. She mounts an ambush rather than hunting so she's a leopard rather than a cheetah. She will, as Isaak Walton accused her 300 years ago, eat ducklings from time to time and even the occasional passing water vole but mostly she concentrates on fish. But her metabolism is efficient. Scientists have shown that a captive 10 pound pike can survive and grow normally on just three and a half times its body weight of food in a year. In the natural state, a pike's annual consumption is probably five to six times its own body weight – so our monster possibly eats a 180 or 200 pounds of fish a year.

She eats only when hungry to satisfy her modest needs. Most of her time she rests, sometimes when the weather is cold, in a virtual comatose torpor. In shallow waters it's possible to find her submerged like a log for days on end. She will move so little that if a strong wind stirs up the silt, it will lay finely over her and she won't even flick a pectoral to shift the sediment. And if you're lucky enough to catch her, on the bank she will be equally quiescent. You might think she is aware of her fate and knows the game is up but much more probable is that the weight of her huge body out of the water makes vigorous movement impossible.

fishes, wherever pike are pressured and caught, damage is done. Man and his fishing tackle are the only combination that can realistically threaten the life of a great female pike and this is what the man who wants monsters must remember. Farm ponds and ditches will have their 10 pounders, perhaps even 20 pounders from time to time if conditions are unexpectedly favorable. But for the monsters, an angler has to look further afield.

It's no surprise that the greatest pike come from the biggest waters. The pike of the Baltic Sea grow enormous, because they always have room to hide both along the endless coastline and around the out to sea islands and plateaux. And they have a never-ending feast laid before them by the Baltic Sea – herrings, mackerel, sea bass, mullet, and codling all provide plentiful, nutritious, easy-to-catch prey for food. In this immense expanse of water our pike simply eats and grows unseen, uncaught, unimagined. It's the same in some of the massive glacial lakes that you can find in Ireland, Scotland, and Alpine Europe. In these long, wide, endlessly deep waters, there is food and anonymity and 50 pounders can exist. Think, too, of the great wilderness lakes in North America and Canada, places almost unfished since the dawn of time. There, too, is where you will find a monster.

She will be beautiful. Her belly is porcelain white and the rich green and yellow markings on her flanks may well be shot with flecks of orange. This wonderful, mottled coloration provides the camouflage she needs to hide unseen amongst the sedge. Like any beauty, her head is striking. Uniquely unforgettable. Her large, unfathomable eyes are set high on the head for forward and upward vision. Her mouth is massive, generous, shovel-shaped, long and wide. It can open so hugely that she can engulf prey-fish a third her size. And that will satisfy her appetite for weeks to come.

Look into her mouth and you will see a terrifying array of teeth. The bottom jaw is rimmed with long, piercing fangs with edges razor-sharp. The roof of her mouth is a forest of smaller but needle-sharp teeth all angled slightly backwards. Any fish grabbed is only going one way and that is down the gullet.

Great female pike can grow enormous. I am desperately fortunate to have seen three 40 pound plus pike in my life but 50, 60, and even 70 pounders, from time to time, exist around the waters of the northern hemisphere. A female pike of this immensity has few enemies. It's possible an otter could do her harm but would struggle to kill her. There's nothing else that can approach her but man. And this is the key to finding the great female pike of our imagination. Wherever man

PIKE FACTS

The ultimate weight of a species is rarely as intriguing as it is with the pike. Anglers for centuries have been obsessed with the search for leviathans. Think of Fred Buller's magnificent book, *The Domesday Book*, of huge captures. What do I think? Well, evidently, a 50 pound pike, whilst being super special is not impossible. I've seen them myself to this weight. My own feeling is that at the right time, in the right place, the right fish could just scrape into the 70 pound region.

November 2007, Southern England.

It had rained endlessly. John Gilman, Ian Miller, Neil Stephens and I are gutted. For weeks we've been longing to fish the river these coming two days but now, because of ceaseless rain, it's all over its valley floor. As a consolation, our keeper tells us we can fish the lakes on the estate but what's in there no one knows, the places are a mystery. It's cold, too cold for cyprinids so we fancy pike. The morning drags on uneventful. Then, around one in the afternoon,

there's a shouting from way, way up the lake where the forest meets the shore. It's uncanny, primeval and we all look at each other, wonderingly. Then we realize Gilman is missing and we run towards the sound.

He's hunched over an enormous pike. He's gibbering that the great fish took his fly off the surface and leapt with it, head shaking so violently the hook hold came away. But no sooner had John recast into the swelling water than the fish rose again and this time, after ten pulsating minutes, she succumbed. And here she is now, an astounding 32 pounds of gorgeously, menacing fish.

Now, it's Saturday the 24th, again a grey, cold day with a bleak wind and occasional spots of rain. We're nursing hangovers. Gilman made sure the night was a party. Then, at 11, Miller's rubber fish imitation is grabbed savagely just a few yards from the shore. Once again, the pike is large. We see her swirling down deep in the crystal water. She weighs 26 and a half pounds. She's sleek, she's svelte, she's stunning. And there's more still to come.

The afternoon is edging to its close. But already, our two days have been a dream. Fish like these are a privilege to witness. But then Stephens shouts from the far side of the lake and in the gloom we see his rod bent double, his reel giving line. Once again, in the clear water we see a fish flash down deep. My God, she's massive! Twice she comes to the net but she dwarfs it, moving away free. The third time, though, she's in and she's ours and she weighs 36 and a quarter pounds. That's three pike for nearly 95 pounds from two waters no one even suspected held a fish. That's the mystery of pike. Look at those fish. That's why they're so high up this 50 List.

BARBEL *Barbus barbus*

Lithe as a Panther

Region: Europe and Eastern Asia

"The best of all I love the barbels because they roll like big brown and white cats upon the golden shallows and sing in the moonlight with the joie de vivre of June. And because, so, they're all Thames to me and wild rose time and the streams running down from the weir."

Patrick Chalmers from At the Tail of the Weir.

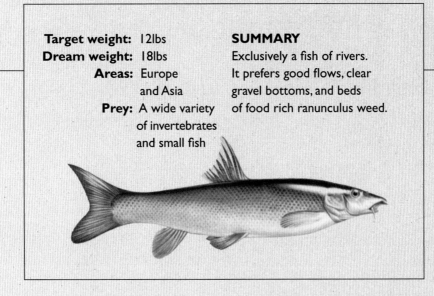

Target weight: 12lbs
Dream weight: 18lbs
Areas: Europe and Asia
Prey: A wide variety of invertebrates and small fish

SUMMARY
Exclusively a fish of rivers. It prefers good flows, clear gravel bottoms, and beds of food rich ranunculus weed.

I couldn't leave the barbel out of the 50 list though there will be game anglers around the world who will wonder why. That's the problem of the list – a fish that is the very breath of life for one angler, can mean next to nothing for another. But this shouldn't be the case. All the 50 have equal merit. If you don't know the barbel, then you should. Look at one. They quiver. Rock hard. Lithe as a panther. Sleek sided. Big finned. Power written in every scale, along every fin ray. Hook a barbel in the flow – and they're exclusively river fish – and you know about it. It's a fish to pull your arm off.

And barbel are clever to a fault. They don't need to know much about you to figure out all about you. In clear water, you can see them sidle up to a bait, nose it, inspect it, sniff it, and reject it. They might be back four or five times over the course of the next hour or two, once again casting a critical eye its way. If you're holding the line, touch legering, you'll feel it happen. You'll know when a barbel comes, lifts the bait tentatively, rolls it round its lips, gives it just a little shake, senses something is amiss, drops it and sidles away.

And, like all the fish in the list, barbel are beautiful. If you barbel fish long enough, you'll notice the endless variety of colors the fish sport. You'll catch them from a pale ivory to a virtual coal-black with every shade in between. You will see oranges, bronzes, golds of all tints. In the rivers of Bohemia, I've seen barbel swimming there almost pure white. Their fins, their pectorals in particular, are almost always coral in color. It's the most tantalizing shade. I can do no better than coral. You'll have to see it for yourself.

And I love the way barbel live their lives. A barbel shoal is a close-knit community. Watch them and you'll see they behave as friends. They love to touch, frequently rubbing bodies together, curling a dorsal fin over the shoulders of a neighbor. Within any shoal, there's a discernible hierarchy: the same fish always lead, the same always follow and the same fish always bring up the rear. And, somehow, barbel pass information between them. For example, a barbel doesn't have to be caught to learn the dangers of tackle and bait. Take a shoal of perhaps 20 fish. If three are caught, the other 17 know what the game is all about. Spooky. Supernatural. But it happens.

Here, I'm going to be controversial. So often, anglers batter barbel into submission. They sit daylong on a known barbel hold and pile in the bait. The barbel senses what's happening but, after hours, they can't resist. The temptation of pint after pint of maggots proves too much. As the sun sets, they give in and they get caught. In the war of attrition, they just get worn down. They're only fish. There are better ways of approaching them.

BARBEL FACTS

• The barbel family is a large one. Most guide books mention at least 12 species. However, a lot of barbel biology is still shrouded in mystery. For example, in Spain, there are at least five species of barbel that are listed virtually nowhere. In the Iberian Peninsular, the comizo can grow huge. Almost certainly, there are 40 and perhaps even 50 pounders to be caught. All this only adds to the mystery and the allure of the fish.

A summer morning. The middle Wye, England. Any year you care to name.

It's good to be up around four a.m. and get down to the river just as early as you can, certainly in the half light. There'll probably be mist in the valley, smoke on the river and dew on the meadows. This is good. If you see any footsteps heading upstream, you go down. It's important to have the river to yourself. You're going to be mobile. You'll fish 20 swims. You'll only make one, perhaps two casts in each place and then move on. You'll be hoping for interest immediately. If not, the barbel aren't at home or they're asleep. You'll be fishing simply, just a lead and a hook on the line. Your bait is a soft cloth bag containing 50 lobworm. You'll be back for breakfast.

You're heading for the beat. A heron lifts up at your approach. A half-eaten chub on the gravel suggests an otter has passed through during the night. You get to the head of the swim, thread on two lobs, flick them into the current and let them trundle down, bouncing the bottom until they reach the shade of the big willow. There's an immediate pull once they settle. You strike. But into thin air. The worms are gone. You move on. Now you're on the Ledge, the place where the river drops from two feet to 20 in the space of a single yard. You know there are fish at the bottom of this riverine cliff and you put on a heavier lead so it falls vertically down through the water column. Over 15 minutes your worms are visited perhaps a dozen times. There are knocks, pulls, tweaks, nudges, suckings, nibbling but there's nothing to strike at. The sun is on the rim of the hills and it's time to move on. You fish the Aquarium, the Steps, the Ship Pool, Green Banks, Wendy's Hole and still you've caught nothing. You hooked one but somehow it shed the hook in its 40 yard run. The Tyre is a long way upstream but it's your best bet.

You wade midway across the river. The mists have dissipated and there's a fine view over a mile downstream. Just standing there, watching the golden water is enough. You can see barbel roll spasmodically all the way down the river, the splashing indicate big fish. There are buzzards in the air. A late to bed badger shuffles along the bank looking for the last lobworm of the night. And, happily, so too is your nine pound barbel. Its pull nearly rips the rod from your hand. The rod's a blur, the line hisses, this is more like it. You're in for a thrilling 10 minutes.

It's a lovely fish. Beaten at last, it lies on its side, the water pushing through its gills, washing down its flanks. In the growing sunlight it simply glows. You unhook your forceps, put them on the shank and simply slide the point free. You right the fish in the current and with a flip of that blood-red tail, the beauty is gone. Eight thirty a.m. so are you. One of life's wonderful mornings.

EEL *Anguilla anguilla*

Fish of Mystery and Magic
Region: North America and Europe – Iceland to the Mediterranean

"Jim phoned me this morning. Yesterday he and his men had been draining the middle pond close to the house with a view to cleaning it out and deepening it. They unearthed a massive eel. According to Jim, they took it into the gardener's potting shed, laid it on the table and measured it, roughly, five feet long. It was thicker than his upper arm he said. Apparently it was still alive but only just. Did I want to see it? Boy, did I want to see it! So I got up there and Jim took me to the shed. But we couldn't find it. We suspected the cats. Or perhaps a fox had got in. And then we came across a trail of slime here and there that led all the way across the lawn, through the meadow of long grass and into the bottom pond. It was a resurrection. The monster had come back to life."

From John Bailey's fishing diary, August, 1986.

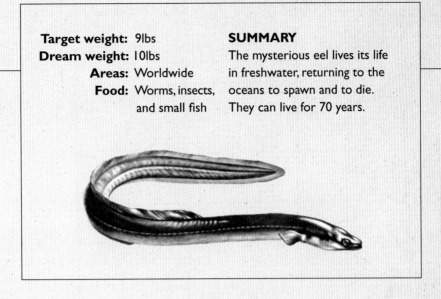

Target weight:	9lbs
Dream weight:	10lbs
Areas:	Worldwide
Food:	Worms, insects, and small fish

SUMMARY

The mysterious eel lives its life in freshwater, returning to the oceans to spawn and to die. They can live for 70 years.

Eels. Fish of mystery and magic. Endless studies have revealed more questions than answers.. That's the appeal. That's why they're in the 50.

My own eeling heaven goes back to the early sixties, to the days before electric bite indicators and my mates and I would fish for eels summer holidays long. Tin foil was our indicator. We'd loop a cylinder of the stuff over the line between the reel and the rod butt and then sit back, blissfully happy, in endless sunlit days, waiting for the fun to start. And here's the fun part. When an eel took, that silver paper would hit the butt with the force of a bullet. The line would hiss out. This was as exciting as anything that had happened to me in the world of fishing. It was the venom of it all. The sheer drama. It didn't really matter if you missed that eel. The run was everything. Galvanizing. A charge of adrenaline that had us whooping.

There was another August day, this time in 1964 when I was fishing a little estate lake. My bait – a chunk of roach – was placed near the single island. It was mid-day and very hot, not what you'd put down as eel weather but the silver paper rattled up and I was into a monster. Yes, a monster. This was the biggest eel I've ever hooked or seen. It might have been as big as Jim's escapee. I don't know. I battled it for half an hour. I was exhausted – I was only a kid – and the eel, in the end, got the better of me. I sat down and I wept.

Since that day, I've had a thing about big eels and Jim himself has kept the passion well-fueled. Jim had a friend, a rich one, whose wife, lavishly bejewelled, fell out of a fishing boat into Loch Ness, Scotland, and drowned. The man had divers look for her body – not out of love but to retrieve the lost jewels. Seems the divers went down once and gave up the quest. The eels that came out of the deep water crevices at them were just too horrendous to face again, whatever the financial compensation. Far

fetched? When I haunted Ness 20 years back, I met two men who swore a 19 foot eel had been caught in the cages surrounding the outflow from the Foyers electrical plant. They were drunk, I was drunk and perhaps the story has been fudged. I care to think not. The Loch Ness monster? You've got my answer.

EEL FACTS

• One of the problems of eel fishing is that the hook is almost invariably swallowed and given the writhing nature of the fish, it's almost impossible to remove. To catch an eel, therefore, is all too frequently to condemn it to death. Surely, in these days of technology, a hook material could be found that would break down in the juices of the fish within a day or two? Then, and only then, would I rig up my eel rods once more!

February, 2008. River Wye, Builth Wells, Wales.

I'm making a film on grayling. It's early in the morning and there's a crackling frost. Last night saw temperatures plummet and the river is smoking in the early morning light. The fishing is desperately slow. The crew and I blame the bone-aching cold of the previous night, but perhaps this is not the cause.

Suddenly, without warning, a huge dog otter heaves a thrashing eel onto an island just the other side of the run I'm fishing, no more than 20 yards away.

The cameraman whoops softly. This is a coup. The eel is being eaten from the tail up. Lashing, writhing, watching itself disappear. I cannot imagine the pain and the horror it is enduring. This is an unspeakable death being enacted in front of us this glorious, God-given day. The recordist is giving me the thumbs up. He can hear the bones crunching on his headset. We've got the sound as well as the action. The eel's backbone is destroyed. Its life is effectively over. But we're close enough to still see the creature twitch in death unending. Eels, heaven help them, have so often met their fate like this. If we do have a life after death, then get praying you come back as the otter.

NILE PERCH
Lates niloticus

The World's Largest Percoid
Region: The Nile and its associated lakes

"The Nile perch is a thoroughly honest fish. Its name tells exactly what it is: a perch inhabiting the Nile, and what a perch! It is by all odds the largest percoid fish through the world. But apart from its size, it differs only slightly from the common perch of Europe and North America — the quarry par excellence of every small boy with a hook, a line, and a worm for bait."

Leander J. McCormick, Game Fish of the World *1949.*

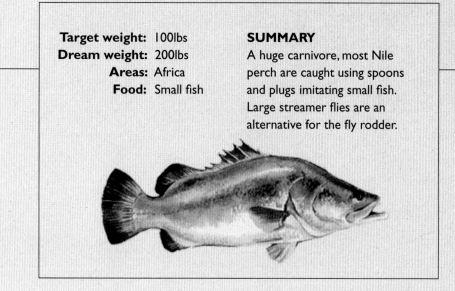

		SUMMARY
Target weight:	100lbs	A huge carnivore, most Nile
Dream weight:	200lbs	perch are caught using spoons
Areas:	Africa	and plugs imitating small fish.
Food:	Small fish	Large streamer flies are an
		alternative for the fly rodder.

Exactly. How many of us started out with the simplest of rods, a fixed line, a worm, and a perch on the end? Multiply everything a hundredfold and you're looking at the Nile perch challenge. My own Nile perching has been disappointingly unadventurous. One guided trip. All mod cons.

Indiana Jones, I think not. But friends have done things far more thrilling. Shirley Deterding, for starters, flew her own light plane into Murchison Falls, under the Ugandan radar. She caught Nile perch there, hooked a crocodile and was lucky to get that plane out intact.

Equally impressive was the epic journey to the same area endured by my Danish friend Jens. Robbers on the bus that took him to the river. Hippos waiting to pounce during the night. Crocodiles everywhere. Tsetse flies. Renegade soldiers. A team of thugs out to murder him. But he escaped and he caught fish and his tale is mesmerizing. So is that of James Ellis. I can't speak highly enough of the man. He's always been tough as teak and the greatest of friends. Several years ago with his then girlfriend, Wendy, Adrian Babault and Chris Trent, he put together a trip to the neglected western shores of Lake Turkana. Nile perch and adventure both were the object of James's mission. You read his words and you look at the photographs and you realize why Nile perch simply bombard their way into the top 50.

NILE PERCH FACTS

• It's often stated that Nile perch aren't great fighters. Sometimes this is true. But not always. Traveler Andy Davison writes, "I proceeded to hang onto some unseen monster with at least a V8 power pack. After five minutes of deep boring runs and with some 200 yards of 30-pound line out, everything went slack. Retrieving the line, I found a kinked wire trace and two hooks straightened out on my Rapala Magnum plug."

Autumn 2004. James Ellis in conversation with JB.

The four of us met at Tom's place where a land cruiser and a Land Rover were waiting, fully equipped with fuel, water, food, outboard boat and engine and all the fishing kit you could ever imagine. This, we told ourselves, was the stuff of adventures.

We all knew that the near 300 mile trip to Turkana itself would be one of the great hurdles and we were to be proved quite right. Tarmac soon gave way to gravel and then even the gravel ran out leaving us to travel on whatever God had laid down. There was no track, no route, no anything. Nobody living could remember an expedition using this particular route so there was no map to draw on. Without GPS we'd have been doomed and as it was, hardly a day ever went wholly right. A lot of our water went bad, probably contaminated through ill-washed storage tanks. Punctures. Paint-stripping miles of thorn-armoured scrubland. Soft sand that sucked one or the other of the vehicles down to the axle. Tribes that were for the most part friendly but, around the border zones where bandit activity increased, you simply could not take safety for granted. Indeed, I spent at the very least one sleepless night as we camped in a dry river valley just listening for sounds, straining my eyes over the moonlit desert around. We all knew deep down that safety wasn't anything we could rely upon in these lonely stretches of no-mans land.

We endured three days of intense heat, dust and danger, running low on water, realising we had little, if any, back up. The landscape was harsh, unremitting and we knew wouldn't give us a simple scrap of sympathy or support if our plans went wrong. And then, just when we were beginning to think Turkana could be nothing but a fantasy, there it was, a mirage shimmering in a fast-approaching distance.

It was evening of the fourth day when we drove finally to the shores, and, you've guessed it, got the land cruiser stuck and managed to puncture one of the Land Rover's wheels. But we were saved: the Turkana people proved to be gems. Thirty of them materialized from nowhere and soon the vehicles were up, running and fit again. In the darkness, local lads guided us and helped set up camp. Their amazement to see us was absolutely profound. Our whole manic quest seem to thrill them to the core and they proved to be a kind, gentle, proud people who could not do enough to help us. In the quietness of that first night, Chris Trent and I took a short walk to the lake and Chris flashed his torch beam out onto the waves. A road of cat's eyes flickered back at us: crocodiles. Legions of them. We retreated, thoughtful, back to our tents, and, believe me, zipped up tight.

The next days were a fisherman's dream. We caught Nile perch, plenty of them and big ones but we'd be the first to admit that our success was down to the generosity of the men, local fishermen, who guided us. Nothing was too much for them: they'd help us set up camp upon camp, day after day. They'd clear the site of stones and usher away the ever-present scorpions. They'd dive deep into the croc-infested waters and free a 30 dollar plug for the reward of a cigarette. They told us of the legends of the lake, initiated us into the lore of that fabulous land. Within days, these fine people had become our rock, our support, our friends.

We caught fish simply spinning off bankside rocks, but best of all were the expeditions out in the boat on the vast waters of the lake, a wary eye always open for quickly-changing weather conditions. Perhaps our greatest day was fishing around the remote central island, rugged, gaunt, lonely and as wild a place as exists on earth. We caught big fish there, hard against the steep cliffs and we photographed them in the gloom of the caverns and fissures that ran deep into the structure of the island itself.

ASP
Aspius aspius

The Greatest of Freshwater Predators

Region: Europe and Western Asia

"Do fishermen come to resemble the fish they fish for? N is dour, bad tempered, snappy, not too bright, and smells rather. He fishes for nothing, absolutely nothing, but pike. D is fun, happy, generous, and there's always a song on his lips. I don't think he's ever fished anything but a dry fly."

John Bailey's fishing diary, **Thoughts on an English Game Fair,** *July 2000.*

Target weight: 7lbs
Dream weight: 15lbs
Areas: Europe and Asia
Food: Small fish and frogs

SUMMARY
The asp is a voracious shoal fish, pursuing its prey in the upper layers of still and running waters.

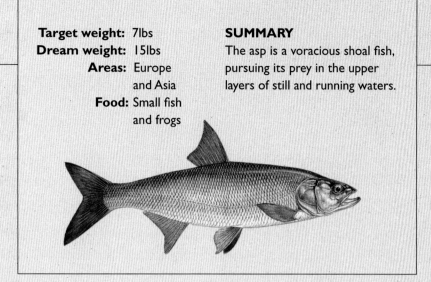

The asp is hard pushed to be included in this sample of freshwater predators where it has serious competition for its place in the 50. I've always had a fancy for North American lake trout. They're a form of char really but they're big and they look mean and if they reflect their surroundings in the least, they must be magnificent. Chris Batin (*Alaska's Trophy Sport Fish*) says, "Pursuing trophy lake trout is not a sport for the faint of heart. It's a gutsy type of angling when the fish is given half a chance to show off its stuff. The laker is gifted with the ability to do underwater what a steelhead is capable of doing above water. I've seen laker's twist, roll, and fight with a vigor that would knock the scales off most other sport fish. Laker's gyrations are like cement mixers, and they have a bulldog tenacity for

staying deep. On many occasions, I've worn out my arms and wrists fishing their springtime feeding frenzies."

Wow! Why aren't they quite in the list then? Well, they're tiptoeing on the fringes and I could say they don't sail in because you fish for them generally trolling or legering a bait. But then again, that's how you fish for ferox trout and they sail in. I guess ferox are just more rare, more secretive, and more of a mystery.

And why have I included pike (*esox lucius*) and even Amur pike in the 50 and not the muskellunge? David Richey, (*How to Catch Trophy Freshwater Game Fish*) says, "Muskies are maniacs. Pure and simple, they are crazy, nuts, impossible to live with, and like a good woman, impossible to live without.

They're unpredictable, belligerent, given to moods of inactivity, and also capable of causing a muskie fever in sportsmen that approaches epidemic proportions." I have an English friend, the Colonel, who has caught two muskies and he agrees with Mr. Richey. However, having caught his two muskies, the Colonel says that he's quite happy to return to his pike fishing which he finds more challenging and more satisfying. As I've never known the Colonel to be wrong about anything piscatorial, I've got to run with his word.

Keith Elliott, and many others, would put up a strong case for the alligator gar. Sorry lads. I don't like his nose. And I don't like the thought he could walk out of the water and chase me around the woods either.

There's a stronger case for the wall-eye and its European and Asian half-brother, the zander. I fished a fortnight on the Volga with Andre, my boatman, who wouldn't catch anything else, even the huge pike and perch that periodically ghosted past. All he wanted to do was jig small dead baits over the stern of the boat. He had the most gentle hands, an exquisite touch. Zander are extremely perceptive for a predator and more frequently than not drop a bait once it's been sampled. Not so with Andre. He turned virtually all the taps into takes. I remember how fabulous

those zander looked – often very big ones – in the light of those Ukrainian sunshine days. And they tasted creamy and steaming, straight from the fire, when we lunched on one of the river's many islands.

It was Andre, during that period, that got me fishing for asp. Now, the asp does just scrape into the 50 largely because you fish for it in such a wide variety of ways. The asp is a game fish, a fish that challenges you. You can fish for it light and you can fish for it with imagination. And Andre showed me one unforgettable evening that cemented my affection for the asp forever.

ASP FACTS

• At first sight, the asp can be mistaken for a chub. But it's a super-charged chub. Whilst chub are predatory, asp are voracious. They'll smash into shoals of prey fish with a volcanic fury about them. And asp, too, grow beyond a chub's wildest dreams. Any man who catches a 10 pound chub is a hero. It's just possible that asp reach three times this size. And, whilst a chub gives a good, bullheaded first run, the asp simply scorches. Hook one on fly gear and the reel is a blur.

July 1998. The Volga. John Bailey's Diary.

I've never seen sunsets like these here in the delta and whilst all I want is a beer Andre insists we get in a boat, leave the mother ship and travel down one of the canals, fast flowing towards the sea. As we chug through the reed marsh, he says he has located a big school of asp. Better. A big school of big asp. And he's right. We turn a bend, the water opens out and as far as you can see, it's being boiled into a frenzy by feeding fish. There are bream and rudd and small carp skittering everywhere. The asp are in the most magnificent feeding overdrive. They're everywhere. Bow waving. Smashing into fish. Cartwheeling out of the water. Asp of eight, ten, perhaps even 15 pounds. My Mepps number 6 is simply hammered after two turns of the reel. Eight pound line. Fizzing clutch. Hooks come free but the lure is taken a second time, almost instantly I retrieve it. This asp is perhaps bigger than the first. It goes crazy in the molten light. It's like a vast lump of burnished gold. Andre's laughing. For once he seems to have forgotten his damned zander. Big asp he's shouting. We celebrate, as ever, with a pull from his vodka bottle. God knows how I survive this place.

BELUGA STURGEON   *Huso huso*

Creatures from the Crack of Creation

Region: Black and Caspian Seas and their inflowing rivers

"Sometimes, on the long row back to the mother ship, I'd see a sturgeon hunting. A beluga, the mother of all the sturgeons. Possibly the most awesome fish on the planet, creatures from the crack of creation. They surged into the shallow water as they hunted, their backs black against the silvery, shivering water."

From Trout at Ten Thousand Feet *John Bailey, 2001.*

			SUMMARY
Target weight:	250lbs		The Beluga is one of over 30
Dream weight:	1,000lbs		sub species in the sturgeon family.
Areas:	Black and		Also a prime angling target is
	Caspian seas		the white sturgeon of North
Food:	Fish		America.

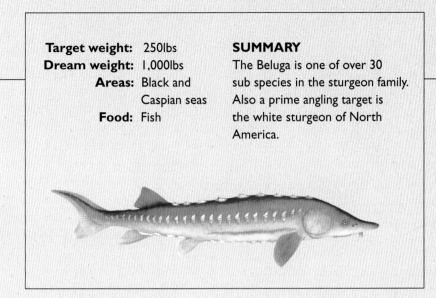

You'll only want to catch one beluga, just to say you've done it, tangled with the biggest, oldest, most hair-raising fish in freshwater. Everything about the beluga sturgeon is outlandish. The fact that they swam the world's waters 60 million years ago. That they mature sexually around 18 years of age and can live for over 100 years. That they can grow in excess of 2,000, perhaps 3,000 pounds in weight. That they are being hunted close to extinction for that fateful cargo of theirs. Their black eggs, their black gold, their caviar, which, as I write in the spring of 2008 is costing $4,800 (£2,470) for just under one ounce (25 grams). That is approximately $975 (£500) for a spoonful.

And, of course, equally startling are the waters that the beluga inhabit. Your best chance today is in the bottom reaches of the Ural River, close to where it feeds the Caspian Sea. This is a flat world of endless marsh and slow, oozing channels as the Ural breaks up into its delta. There are few people in this vast waterland – some fisher folk, some reed cutters, river guards… and caviar bandits. This is the frontline of the caviar war. Protecting these goliaths as they roll in from the Caspian is one of the crucial jobs in world conservation today. Heavy Mafia involvement makes it dangerous. This isn't always a place to be angling!

The time to go is May. Then the cyprinids – carp, asp, and bream – are spawning in the endless Ural reed beds and the sturgeon leave the sea to hunt them. Just to watch is enough. Pods of these great fish heave themselves over the sand bars and plough up the muddy channels, raiding as they go. You can hear fish before you see them. A sturgeon attack is like a bomb being dropped – most fish weigh in excess of 200 pounds. Many are 400 pounds and over. A few top the 1,000 pound mark. These are not fish that are easy to miss!

Fishing for them isn't easy to forget. A typical day will see you and your guide set out after breakfast, probably in a boat that's seen better days with an engine kept going entirely by Kazakh ingenuity. Your guide will have bait for you – asp are best, four pound fish cut into eight ounce or one pound chunks. The lead will be heavy, the gear monumental and you'll relax as you cruise through the marshes.

Your guide will moor you in the midst of spawning fish for there you know the sturgeon will congregate. You'll see the belugas head up the flow towards you. Their backs break surface – you see the great scales, the scoots, glisten as they emerge. Sometimes a head comes clear as a mouth searches for an airborne carp. The water is like chocolate and fish nudge into your boat, swimming underneath it, lifting it nearly clear of the surface. You cannot believe that there are fish so huge, so numerous. As you lower your lump of bait into the current your heart is beating to bursting point. The blood is flooding your temples. You're dry-mouthed, sick with apprehension, praying almost that the line will not tighten.

But it will. You will feel the bodies of the passing fish brush on the line. You imagine them snouting in the bottom mud, following the smell of blood from your bait.

You can feel that lump of asp being inspected, picked up, swallowed. The line draws tight. The reel begins to click. You strike and 10 yards away the great battleship of steel-grey fish levers itself up and out into the Kazakh sunshine. It hangs, glistens, and falls back with a force that threatens to swamp your boat.

Believe me, if that fish weighs 250 pounds or so, the next 30 minutes will be hell for you. It's you against a fish near double your own weight. The sturgeon can run you down to the spool. It might jump another dozen times. By the time you get it to your boat, you will be gasping for the pain to be over. You'll curse the heat of the sun and the sweat streaming down your back. You'll sob with relief when Sasha bends over the boat and levers the hook out so that the beluga can swim free. He dips his finger in the Ural and in water writes the figures 140 – 140 kilos. This is a ritual that you will celebrate long into the night to come.

BELUGA FACTS

• Guryev is the center of operations and has the nearest major airport. Check travel and safety issues very, very carefully. Double check visas, finances and inoculations with a fine-tooth comb.

• Uptide nine or 10 foot rods are ideal with a casting weight of six to 10 ounces. Multiplier reels are essential – Ambassador 10,000s take some beating. Owner 8|0 hooks are obligatory. Use a 50 pound line with a 15 to 20 foot long, 100 pound leader.

March 2004, Ural River, Kazakhstan.

JJ and I decide on a crazy plan. We anchor for three hours in one of the deepest of the channels, a body of water where we have been seeing the biggest of the beluga. Fish after fish bulldozes past but we do nothing. Then Johnny points. Here comes the fish of our dreams. A sturgeon a yard across the shoulders, very possibly more. She's a behemoth of a beluga. She trucks up the river towards us and prey fish shower like confetti before her.

The sturgeon is five yards from our boat and JJ swings out a dead, hooked-up carp. It lands perhaps a meter from the great fish's head and, in frozen time, the fish senses it, rears up, inspects it and swallows it down. JJ waits. Nothing happens. Then he strikes once, twice and still nothing happens. Slowly, the whole river begins to move as the hooked beluga gradually levers herself around, changes direction and heads off back to the vastness of the sea.

This is our plan, we fire the engine and we follow. Within half an hour we've reached the sandbars that signal the end of the river, we're over them, we're into the sea, into a shimmering cauldron of heat. For three hours, we follow the great fish as it swims steadily south. We lose all sense of time, of space, of reality. We're never more than 10 yards away from the fish, sometimes we're all but parallel with it. Its eye is like a saucer. Its snout is as long as a man's arm.

The sun is settling in the sky and Sasha powers up the boat, cuts the line close to the fish's head and with a swirl, the fish is gone. "Iran," he says. He bends down, wets his finger and writes 850 on the gunnel. We've been following a fish of 2,000 pounds for five ridiculous hours. Three men destroyed by a fish.

CATFISH

CATFISH

WELS AND OTHERS *Silurus glanis*

The Big Whiskered Scavengers

Region: Throughout the world

"A goonch, the guides all said in unison, pointing at the vast, black shape sliding across the gravels towards our raft. It was coming fast but we still watched it for a full 30 seconds before it passed underneath us, its bulk actually lifting us six inches higher in the water. Then it was off, lot in the deep water. Seven, perhaps eight feet long. At least 18 inches across the back. Awesome."

From John Bailey's Nepal diary, 1992.

Target weight: 80lbs
Dream weight: 150lbs
Areas: Worldwide
Food: Fish and frogs

SUMMARY
Catfish are generally scavengers on the waters' bed but they will hunt fish in the upper zones. Worldwide there are over 30 families of freshwater and marine catfish.

Catfish make the 50 because of their bulk, because of their enormity. The leviathan members of the catfish family worldwide are monsters both in size and in looks and it's this dark appeal that makes them so attractive. The goonch of the northern Indian/Himalayan region is particularly impressive in its dragon-like way. In pools off the Karnali River, in Nepal, I've seen them lying in the shallows looking like submerged tree trunks. The tales have it that dead animals are thrown in as bait, a village dog perhaps or a cat – and when a monster is hooked on a rope for a line, the whole village assist in pulling the beast ashore. I can't vouch for these tales. Only that the fish are immense.

The world knows more about the Wels catfish, the giant of western Europe, Russia and the fringes of Asia. Again, this huge fish attracts tales to it that could well be apocryphal. When I traveled the Balkans before the disastrous wars of the 1990s, I heard many such. One Albanian was fishing a lake for catfish with a live carp strapped to a thin leather thong which was tied to his wrist. The catfish took, pulled him in and forced him down to the depths. A few days later, both fish and man were found washed up in a cove. The catfish weighed twice as much as its would-be captor. I don't know. You decide.

As I write, it's the catfish of the River Ebro in north eastern Spain which are attracting the headlines. Fish to well over 200 pounds exist here. It's in Russia on the River Volga and its delta that I've done most of my travelings with the species. In 1995, I was a member of a group living on an island in waters that had once belonged to Soviet party chiefs. This fact didn't make the accommodation particularly salubrious. You could smell the single toilet at 100 paces. The fishing, though, was extraordinary. Occasional Beluga sturgeon would plough past. There were asp, carp, perch, tench, roach, rudd and, of course, Wels catfish. It was these that we were primarily targeting.

Dawn was the time to be out. The island was surrounded by a maze of channels as the Volga divided and subdivided. Each of these channels might easily be 100 yards across, many feet deep and moving with huge speed and muscularity. The fishing was necessarily by boat, mostly guided by a boatman heavy with hangover. The techniques weren't particularly pretty either. The guides almost insisted that we used huge frogs as bait, fished live, hooked behind the neck, and cast down into the depths. The rod tips would nod in a metronomic fashion until the poor beasts were taken. They'd be taken with a savagery which would leave you in no doubt that things were afoot.

Still, those mornings had a charm of their own. The sunrises were magical. The light behind the avenues of poplars would grow in intensity and the great oily river before us would, eventually, burst into bubble-spangled life. The catfish threw up vast sheets of bubbles, the size

of tennis courts as they rummaged for their breakfast. Birdlife was exuberant: bitterns boomed from distant reed beds. And, as the mornings wore on, the river would become busy with passing traffic. Boats laden with reeds cut for thatchers around Europe sometimes filled the rivers.

The current way out would be too strong to fish effectively and we'd moor in great eddies and fish the slow-moving slacks. Occasionally catfish would come to the surface to hunt, massive things, mouths like tunnels. But generally, our frogs would be taken down deep and we'd brace ourselves for a half hour battle with fish that fought like animated bags of cement.

The most exciting battle I witnessed was on a later trip, in June 2005. Two Ukrainians were fishing for carp when a Wels chanced upon one of the boily-baited hooks. The fish fought for two hours. It fought through a rainstorm. It fought while the sun sank from high in the sky to beneath the horizon. It fought as the shadows lengthened. It looked as though it was going to fight all night but, eventually it was beached and weighed at over 100 pounds. You couldn't call the fish beautiful. It had leeches two and three inches long glued to its head, waving frantically, Medusa-like. The coarse, mottled skin. The hideous, waving feelers, two feet long perhaps. The tiny, piggy eyes, glaring with hate.

CATFISH FACTS

• If you believe the stories, the goonch can approach 1,000 pounds in weight. The Brahmaputra and its tributaries are noted for big fish. The Karnali is also another important location. There are many catfish species. The other one notable for its size is the Mekong catfish. All evidence suggests that these are now a rare beast indeed due to over-fishing. A friend of mine has spent a year on the Mekong and its tributaries searching for one of its catfish. He failed totally.

June 2005. Volga River, Ukraine.

After breakfast, I meet up with R – the baron of what tourism there is in these parts. He sends his boat and a man to collect me and we speed through the maze of waterways to his camp on an island. It's plush. We have vodka (of course) and he feeds me a quite delicious perch pie. The man is a mine of information about the Volga and the delta. It seems he has camps spread up and down the river for a length of more than 500 miles. The stories he tells are mouth-watering but, of course, he's out to impress and I wonder about their veracity.

Catfish, he says. Easy. Follow me. We wander outside to a large boat bay where 30 or so fishing skips are at their moorings. There are three asp on the boards of one of them. He picks up the first one – it's about four pounds – and lobs it some 15 yards out. It sinks perhaps two feet when two massive shapes emerge underneath it, both of them grabbing and tugging at the dead fish. Wels.

Each well over 100 pounds. He throws a second in the same direction but much closer in. A Wels of perhaps 120 or 130 pounds appears and engulfs the fish like a trout taking a buzzer. The third asp he simply drops down the side of the boat basin at our feet. The fish tumbles and twists for three, four, perhaps five feet down and a similar huge, black shape emerges to swallow it. R looks at me content. "Catfish no problem" he says.

91

ARAPAIMA OR PIRARUCU *Arapaima gigas*

The Rarest of Them All

Region: The Amazon

"The giant pirarucu is, in many respects, an extremely important animal, and yet it is practically unknown outside the areas where it is indigenous. This is all the more remarkable since it occupies a special niche in dictionaries, encyclopedias and general books on ichthyology, being usually described as the largest of freshwater fish. The arapaima belongs to the ancient order of Isospondyli, which also includes the herrings, tarpons, salmons, and trouts, but in appearance it differs greatly from any of these. To a visitor from the north it recalls some prehistoric creature, with its sinister, depressed snout and peculiar arrangement of dorsal and anal fins grouped together so unexpectedly close to its tail. The fish has a long, sub-cylindrical body that is covered with large olive-green scales, which shade from very dark on the back to very light on the belly. Beginning about halfway along the body these scales are tinged at the rear edges with a vivid red hue which suffuses them more and more until towards the tail they have become almost entirely scarlet. It is from this color that the pirarucu gets its name. In the Tupi language 'pira' means fish, while 'urucu' is the name of a bush bearing flame-red seeds."

Leander J. McCormick, Game Fish of the World, 1949.

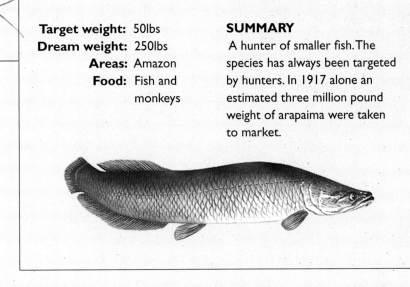

Target weight: 50lbs
Dream weight: 250lbs
Areas: Amazon
Food: Fish and monkeys

SUMMARY

A hunter of smaller fish. The species has always been targeted by hunters. In 1917 alone an estimated three million pound weight of arapaima were taken to market.

The arapaima – and I will call it that because that is the name I've grown up with – is an almost legendary creature today. It always was because of its remoteness. It always will be now because of its rarity. Evidently, in its strongholds deep within the Amazon Basin, the huge arapaima was once a common beast. Today that is not the case.

I only know of three men and a woman, personally, who have tangled with arapaima. They're all friends. I admire them all greatly. Here, in embryo, are their stories.

Simon and Sally Channing spent weeks in the Amazonian rainforest several years ago hunting arapaima.

As far as I'm aware, their complete story has never been told. What I am aware of, however, is that their dedication was immense. This was a period of enormous storms which made the dangers and difficulties even more immense. When they did catch arapaima, it was a colossal testament to their dedication, their courage, and their skill. I'm not surprised about this. I traveled with Simon Channing extensively in the mid 1990s and was always hugely impressed by his sheer durability and good humor. What is typical of Simon is his reluctance to claim any glory and his insistence on making light of the dangers.

Keith Elliott is the angling correspondent for *The Independent on Sunday* and runs the important magazine, *Classic Angling*. Keith, superficially, is possibly a less-easily recognizable adventurer than Simon. He's somewhat older, a little more rounded and hugely cerebral. But he's tough as teak. His own journey, to Ecuador, took place over 20 years back and it was draining. "The mosquitoes were absolutely horrendous so I slept in my bag, preferring the desperate heat to the damage I would otherwise face. In fact, one man who slept near-naked was bitten 189 times on a single leg…in a clearing ahead of us, on the ground, lay what looked like a very large stick. In fact it was a fer-de-lance – one of the most dangerous snakes in the world and the only snake to give chase! Fernando, our guide, crept up on it and killed it with a stick. It was around nine feet long and Vic Sampson put it round himself and said that he was going to take it back, skin it and use it for a belt. Soon we were back in camp and the snake was hanging over a branch. We were drinking and chatting when one of us simply froze. He pointed to the snake. It was slithering down the tree and made off into the jungle. Vic looked decidedly pale…we came back to camp to find a tarantula catching moths in the lamplight outside out tent… there were vampire bats everywhere…"

Talking to both Simon and Keith a would-be arapaima hunter realizes that water depth is pretty well everything. When the Amazon and its tributaries are high, then the hopes of catching arapaima decrease considerably. What you need is the lowest water level possible. When this is the case, huge, shallow lagoons are formed, cut off from the river. It's in these large pieces of stagnant water that arapaima become marooned and catchable. When the river is 16 or 20 feet up, location is just too big a job to contemplate. And, in high water levels, landing an arapaima, too, is virtually impossible. There are too many fallen trees to contemplate a long and ultimately successful battle.

Many years ago, I recall seeing a film – though not professionally made – of some Europeans fishing a lagoon like I've just described, deep in the jungle, for arapaima. Two or perhaps three fish were hooked. One was actually brought into the shallows. They were all big fish.

They were taken on lures and live baits both. It was an extraordinary piece of footage.

Mick Bay is the fourth person with whom I've traveled and fished and he has mounted at least one arapaima search. Mick, rather like Keith, you wouldn't judge to be an Indiana Jones from his appearance alone. Like Keith, Mick is around 60 years old, loves his coffee and cigars but get him into the wilderness and he comes alive. I've traveled with him in India and Greenland and he's a rock. He also concurs with everything that's been said so far. He made it plain to me that location is the basis of any success story. Obviously, looking at the Amazon and its catchment area is a huge task in itself. When the waters are high, it becomes impossible. And, above all, Mick emphasized that through much of its range, the arapaima has been hunted near to extinction.

ARAPAIMA FACTS

• Probably the most successful arapaima session ever took place in 1913 when a party led by Sir Walter Egerton, with two rods angling at a time, succeeded in catching seven arapaima in two and a half hours. The scene was a pool on the Simoni, a small tributary of the River Rupununi in what was then British Guyana. Tarpon gear was used and pieces of dead bait went on the hook.

February 2008. In conversation with Mick Bay

We eventually found what we were looking for, a large, shallow lagoon which we first thought to be completely remote. But when we finally made it there we found we were not on our own. There were several natives present, all with large nets and dug-out canoes. Quite evidently they had the run of the place. It's important to realize that the arapaima must come to the surface quite frequently to take in lungfuls of air. It's this characteristic that clearly leads regularly to its downfall. What the native fishermen were doing was simple and effective.

As soon as an arapaima showed itself, the natives would lay netting down to cut off a segment of the lake far from the swirling fish. The area the arapaima had to move around in was, effectively halved. When it showed again, once more, they staked netting out to seal off another large area of available water. Now the arapaima's territory was cut down by another 40 or 50 percent. And so it went on throughout the day. Every time the arapaima showed, the nets came closer and closer to it, forcing it increasingly into a corner, a small bay in the lagoon.

It was there that the end came. With clubs and spears and with a huge thrashing of water, the arapaima, a very large fish, was killed. It was off to market. Of course, the whole purpose of the trip for us was wasted but at least, I'd seen my fish.

BARRAMUNDI

Scleropages leichardt

The Giant Perch of the East

Region: North Australian coast, Asia coast as far as China

"Blown away by the fish market. Spent hours there. Couldn't drag me away. All manner of jacks, snapper-like fish, sharks, mullets, squids, octopuses. But best of all was what they said was a barramundi. A great silver fish. Even in death these were impressive. Fifty pounds. Perhaps more. Those bright, hard, silver scales. The dramatic fins. Something riveting about the eye. A fish to tangle with. I made a mental note."

From John Bailey's Fishing Diary, 1989. India's East Coast.

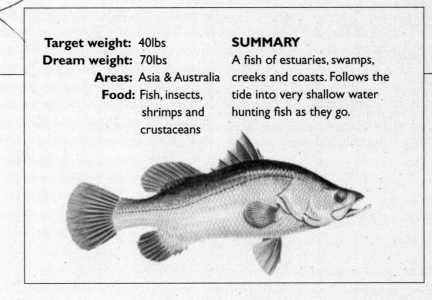

Target weight: 40lbs
Dream weight: 70lbs
Areas: Asia & Australia
Food: Fish, insects, shrimps and crustaceans

SUMMARY
A fish of estuaries, swamps, creeks and coasts. Follows the tide into very shallow water hunting fish as they go.

I've tried to catch barramundi on a good few occasions. Sometimes around the coast of India, but I've failed. To be honest, despite what I've been told, I'm not sure I've been close to fish, even if they'd been there. I've also tried on the east coast of Australia but I don't think I got far enough north, in truth. Perhaps that's been my problem: perhaps my failure is that I've always been on the fringe. But in Australia, I did see them live, in Sydney Aquarium.

Again, I was blown away. There was something about them that didn't look real. It was as though they were computer-generated models of fish. Perhaps they looked a little like the tarpon – so silver and solid that they're more like metal than flesh. Those barramundi could swim through a brick wall if they wanted.

I know people who have caught barramundi, of course, and they're adamant that the "barra" goes high in the list of 50. They love their bullishness, their aggression, their fighting abilities. Bait, lure or fly, everyone seems to rate the 'barra' way, way up the scale. Neill Stephen is one of the brave breed of world travelers, a man obsessed with the fish and the adventures angling can offer the open minded.

BARRAMUNDI FACTS

• The barramundi lives in rivers, creeks and mangrove swamps and spawns in the estuaries and coastal waters both. It can reach, abnormally, 100 pounds plus and feeds on crabs, small fish, shrimps and insects. It is closely related to the Nile perch, the legendary African freshwater fish. The barramundi is common around Asian coastal regions, throughout the Indian Ocean and even as far as the shores of China and the Pacific. It is also common throughout New Guinea and the northern coastline of Australia.

From Neill Stephen's Australian Journal, 2007.

I'm in the Kimberley region in the northwest of Australia. Forget Bondi Beach and Ayers Rock, this is Australia's last area of true wilderness, untamed and harsh, a place where a failed engine or an empty water bottle can easily turn you in into an undiscovered pile of bones. The heat is alien and so are the landscapes, lonely baobab trees and red mountains, kangaroos and ancient aboriginal cultural sites. And best of all, for the fisherman, water everywhere. This is monsoon land and as a result covered in a vast coral fan of rivers, creeks and swamps. The choice is dazzling, from shallow, fast streams to giant muddy, tidal sweeps, from placid, lily-strewn waterholes to desert stranded billabongs. The barramundi whilst spawning in the estuaries, makes its way far inland to feed and can be found in all of these environments. A good guide will take you through most of them in a day. The humidity makes visiting in the wet season almost impossible but if you dare try it, you are in for a treat as new rivers appear overnight, dramatic waterfalls form and the saltpans open out into giant lakes.

But for me, the most exciting way to catch the 'barra' is to wait at the top of one of the smaller rivers for the fish to come in with the tide. It's what I'm doing now. The water is little more than a trickle, it resembles a Highland stream with shallow rock pools and stranded shoals of mullet. But now, right in front of my eyes, the tide begins to flood over the rocks and the whole atmosphere changes. The mullet know it and become more agitated and it's not long before I hear the first 'barra' crash under the far bank signalling the start of the action. Places like this are hard to find but they're awe-inspiring, the water running wide and powerful through deep, red mountain gorges. The water is like a primeval soup, mud brown and bath warm, absolutely teeming with life. All around big saltwater crocs are bathing on the mud-banks, ominously slipping in as I approach. The chances are that if I hook into a fish and play it overlong all I will do is attract the attentions of shark or croc or both.

The fishing is based around working structures that 'barra' love. I'm looking typically for sunken trees, for the mangrove roots and the creek mouths here. My nerves are jangling as I flick a lure up a narrow inlet, drawing it back under the mangrove roots, waiting for the violent hit of a taking 'barra'. These are fish that take no prisoners. Once you hook them they go ballistic in a series of deep, crashing jumps. No wonder they're Australia's top sport fish.

Rachaela is into a small one, I suppose, but even so, it fights furiously, more airborne than water-based. It's a wild, exciting fight and in the heat, draining, too. Out of the water, even a small fish is impressively handsome, almost prehistoric. Big silver scales. Deep humped back. A spiked dorsal and the scooped forehead ending in that cavernous, bristling mouth. Like all the serious fish on the planet, this one is synonymous with its environment. It's a predator that has been carved through the ages into an emblem of its habitat. The average size of fish here is six to eight pounds perhaps but there's every chance of fish over 30 and sometimes way over that. A fish like Rachaela's is a delicacy. Taking one like this will do no harm whatsoever to the stocks. An Aussie basket of 'barra' and chips with a cold beer at the end of the day will just lift this session into the realms of perfection.

CARP
Cyprinus Carpio

Eggheads of the Fishy World

Region: Throughout the world

The Fisherman's Tables – Carp. One day equals 18 hours.
Eighteen hours equal one potato. Ten years equals one carp.

H. T. Sheringham

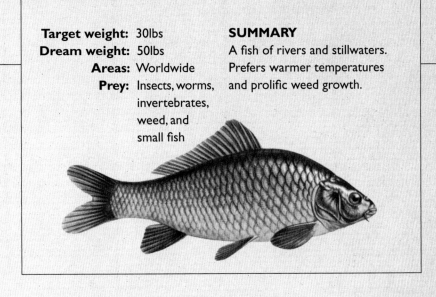

Target weight: 30lbs
Dream weight: 50lbs
Areas: Worldwide
Prey: Insects, worms, invertebrates, weed, and small fish

SUMMARY
A fish of rivers and stillwaters. Prefers warmer temperatures and prolific weed growth.

Sheringham, angling editor of *The Field* magazine, back early in the last century, got it right. Carp are in the 50 because of their brain power. They are the eggheads of the fishy world. Of course, 100 years ago when Sheringham wrote, carp were even more difficult to catch before the advent of modern baits, methods, and tackle. A parboiled potato then was seen as a prime carp bait. And, really, they hated them! Your potatoes could grow old and rot on the lake bed before a carp would even sniff at them.

In some ways, I'm not the right guy to be writing this piece on carp simply because I so dislike the modern carp scene. As I see it now, it's dominated by quick fixes and shortcuts. Any method will do, providing it lands a carp. Anglers have become obsessed with size. Size in this twilight world of the modern carp fisher equals fame. And fishing isn't about fame.

The problem is that modern carp fishing has become like an arms race. A method and a bait are tried and the carp quickly suss it out and have the upper hand. The anglers think of a new approach and, for a moment, they begin to win. The carp then solve this new problem and they become unconquerable until the next trick is devised and so it goes. *Ad infinitum*. Perhaps, in the end, the anglers will just run out of tricks and the carp will eventually reign supreme. I hope so.

Of course, you can't blame the carp for any of this. You can't hold their size and good looks and general overall desirability against them. And, indeed, there have been carp in my life of whom I've become hugely fond. Take Herman as a prize example.

Herman lived in a rather dingy pond down in the south of England for many years. He was rightly feted, a hugely impressive, fully scaled common carp, and a character that outwitted 99 percent of the anglers who pursued him. This is what amazed me about Herman. He lived in little more than a duck pond, a puddle of probably less than an acre. And, at any given time, there might be 20 anglers fishing for him, all with two rods. Imagine it. That little water would be dissected by 40 or more lines, cutting through it like cheese wires. There would be baits everywhere lying temptingly amidst mountains of loose offerings.

How would Herman have spent his days and nights? Presumably, sidling around, back to the bank, testing every morsel of food he thought about sucking into his mouth. What a life of infinite caution he must have led. Surely there must have been times when he thought, 'Hang it, let them catch me, can I really be bothered.' But no, he didn't do that. He maintained his concentration levels to an incredibly focused degree. When he died, the anglers mourned and went elsewhere. For all I know, the fishery owner went broke.

I spent years trying to catch Eric from a small gravel pit some 15 miles from my house. I think I began to try to catch him in about 1973 and I gave up trying to catch him when he died in the later eighties. Sometimes, I would spend every evening throughout the summer trying to catch Eric. Every day I'd see him. It was like I was part of his life, like the postman arriving or the milkman coming to our door. After saying hello, he'd ignore me. Almost always. There was just one night when he gave me a flicker of hope. For a first time he began to take my floating baits from the surface, one by one, with complete absence of caution. He was so close, he was so greedy, he was so near to being mine. And you know, I bottled it. I don't know what possessed me. With a complete failure of nerve, with my prize so close, I packed and went home. My decision, in part, baffles me to this day.

I well remember the Buddha. This fish, possibly, was even larger than Eric and lived in the tiniest of pools in the grounds of a friend of mine, only a couple of miles away from where I now write. Perhaps the Buddha's pond was half an acre, no more. It was always well weeded and the Buddha would wallow in the exact mid-point of the water, always visible, always smiling, always uncatchable. Once again, I never got a bait near the Buddha's mouth. An otter killed him with a chunk out of the throat some three or four years back, so I'll never catch him now.

Perhaps my dearest carp water was my beloved Boathouse Lake. What joys I've experienced there. The carp – before otters got them, too – were massive. And clever. In the last five years of fishing there, I never landed a single one. This never put me off fishing there, probably the reverse. The fact that these great fish swam totally free in their own world impressed me, seemed just, made them fabulous.

CARP FACTS

• Carp are as at least widely spread around the world as brown trout. I can think of countries without them but there aren't many. Because of their tendency to over breed in warm, shallow, fertile waters there are places on the planet where they've become a pest. Carp, therefore, as a family, are at very low risk. Wild carp and crucians, however, are a different matter altogether. These smaller, older, more vulnerable varieties have been edged out of much of their former territory.

August 2007. Wood Pigeons Lake, England.

It's an exquisite day. The sun is beaming through the stately trees, glancing off the big lake in front of me. I'm in thick reed beds, looking hard into the clear water. It's four feet deep. There are six wonderful fish feeding. I put in sweet corn and worms and hemp and they're on the bait, on their heads, tails breaking the surface sometimes, the bottom fizzing. These are wild carp. They've been here decades. They're not the biggest fish I've ever seen or caught but they're untouched, virgin, beautiful.

And I'm float fishing. Is there a better way to fish for carp? I'm so close to the fish that I know I'm going to catch one and I do. The float has gone and so have 50 yards of line in a trice. It's not going to break me, it only weighs about seven pounds but in the sun, with the water lapping at its scales, this is a treasure of a fish. It's almost exactly like one I caught here, in this exact same spot in the reeds, some 40 odd years ago. Perhaps it is the same fish. Or its grandchild. It's wonderful to find waters and fish stocks frozen in time. I'd love to come back when I'm truly old and catch perhaps this carp's grandchild. Perhaps it will be the last fish I'll catch. And I'd be happy with that.

CHAPTER 2
SEA FISHING

SAILFISH _Istiophorus paltypterus_

Aerial Fighter

Region: Worldwide in warm seas

"The sailfish is one of the most beautiful and exotically colored of all game fish. The sight of a sailfish running just below the surface with his sail set, glistening and yet part of the surrounding ocean color, can never be forgotten. Striking, feeding a freshly-hooked fish as scintillatingly alive with colors of deep, dark blue on the back and silver below, vertically barred and spotted with light powder blue and lavender bars."

From Game Fish of the Pacific _by Peter Goadby, **Fifty Edition**, 1987._

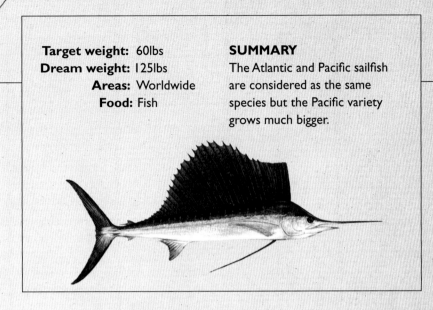

Target weight: 60lbs	**SUMMARY**
Dream weight: 125lbs	The Atlantic and Pacific sailfish
Areas: Worldwide	are considered as the same
Food: Fish	species but the Pacific variety
	grows much bigger.

I'm squeamish about some big game fishing. Often, it seems to me that it's the captain and the crew that do the work and the main thing the angler has to have is money. Some big game fishing, too, demands tackle that is unreasonably heavy and methods that are obviously lacking in skill. Sailfish, however, aren't leviathans. Those of the Pacific are bigger than those found in the Atlantic but even then, they rarely weigh more than 100 or so pounds. This means that, well as they fight, they can be pursued with reasonably light, sensitive tactics. The sailfish is a great aerial fighter, jumping spectacularly. However, because of their light build, they do tire fairly quickly and even their fast runs aren't generally particularly far in extent. Hemingway loved the species. He boated one of 119 and a half pounds off Key West, a big fish that could never go into the record books because Hemingway had had to take the rod from a guest who was suffering.

Shirley Deterding is a sportswoman Hemingway would look at, recognize and instantly admire. She's an artist, a shot, a stalker but, above all, a fisherwoman. She's had several Atlantic salmon over 40 pounds on the fly. She's fished in Mongolia and had massive taimen. She's been to Argentina and landed enormous sea trout. In the darkest days of Ugandan politics, she flew in illegally by light plane to catch mammoth Nile perch. This woman is afraid of nothing. If this woman wants to do something, she does it. That's what Hemingway would adore. So, when she went sailfishing out of Guatemala, Shirley told the crew she wanted to catch on the fly. Despite protests, that's what she did.

SAILFISH FACTS

• It was with sailfish that conservation techniques were pioneered many years ago. Due to the work of three sportsmen from Palm Beach over 80 percent of the sailfish are being released and all of the boatmen and anglers are co-operating by cutting the light, leader wire near the hook if they cannot get the hook out of the fish. This does not harm the sailfish as the hook wears out amazingly soon.

February 2006. Guatemala. From Shirley Deterding's Diary.

I don't care what the boys say, I'm going to use the fly a 10-weight outfit and a strong tippet and strong leader should do the job. And the fly's enormous. It looks like bait anyway. I think they're worried about my casting, the wind, the pitch and roll of the boat but I assure them that they'll be okay. We set out.

And out go the teasers and I watch them way out the stern. I'm getting good at this. I see a sailfish coming in even before the captain. I'm screaming at the boys to pull the teasers in and I see the sailfish it's a big one blushing as it circles, attacking, fired up with excitement. But so are we all.

The cast has gone exactly right, perfectly into the path of the fish. We're all watching. It sees it. But sailfish have brilliant eyesight and the water's crystal. It's not sure. I know I've got to retrieve perfectly, convincingly, goading it into an attack. It's coming. It's coming, it's going over the fly and I know a strike now will be useless. I count one, two, three and as the word four is forming, I see the fish turning right, so I power the strike hard to the left.

It's running hard. I've got to stop it from sounding, I've got to keep it on the surface because my gear isn't strong enough to pull a fish up from deep. It's running now at enormous speed. Our boat's slammed into reverse and the sea's slopping all over the stern. I'm soaked. That's close, I'm nearly pulled overboard. I'm not in a chair but free-standing and one of the boys has his arms round my waist, holding me on the deck. You could forget to breathe it's all that exciting. I know I've got to put every bit of pressure on this fish that I possibly can. You can't let a sailfish fight too hard, too long in water as warm as this. I've got to make sure it lives, it's not stressed, it's not easy prey for sharks. Again, it tries to go deep but I simply pile on the pressure. My arms are bursting but I stop it. It's back on the surface. My God, It's awesome, it's beautiful the guys are saying now that it could be a record for a woman on the fly but a photograph's all I'm willing to risk. Weighing a fish in heat like this is too big a risk. You couldn't forgive yourself for killing a beauty like this...

HALIBUT *Hippoglossus stenolepis*

The Massive Flat Fish

Region: North Pacific and North Atlantic

"I would probably have been happy with flounders for many more years but for a film deemed educational that I saw at school. It was about the commercial line fishermen who sailed out of Aberdeen on the east coast of Scotland. They went north to the White Sea and the film showed them shooting 10-mile-long lines marked by huge orange buoys. There was some irrelevant scenic stuff, but the real thing started when they began to haul the line. A big gaping cod came up first, then some unfamiliar Arctic species. Then the winch began to labour. The camera was focused over the lurching rail and there in the clear cold water was a breath-stopping sight. It was a vast flounder, or so I thought, bigger than the dining table at home, a huge and mighty flounder that must have weighed 200 pounds. Amazingly, the commentator's voice did not rise to a hysterical screech. Instead, it noted calmly, 'The great halibut of northern waters fetches top prices on the Aberdeen fish market…' It was the best afternoon I ever spent at school."

From I Know a Good Place, *Clive Gammon, 1989.*

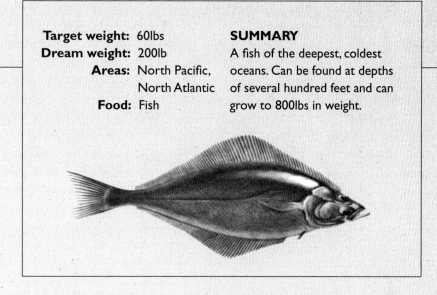

Target weight: 60lbs
Dream weight: 200lb
Areas: North Pacific, North Atlantic
Food: Fish

SUMMARY
A fish of the deepest, coldest oceans. Can be found at depths of several hundred feet and can grow to 800lbs in weight.

Like Clive, and what an endearing and inspirational man he is, flounders have always been dear to me. I first came across them in 1966 down in Mudeford Harbour on the south coast of England. Knowing my absolute yearning to fish the Royalty on the Hampshire Avon, my parents booked the annual holiday there. From 1st to 15th June. We were to leave exactly one day before the season there started! Obviously, I was bereft. Obviously, I had to find alternatives and the flounders of Mudeford, England,

proved up to the task. All right, they weren't the six pound chub, the two pound roach, and the 10 pound barbel I'd dreamed of. But at the age of seven or eight, even at around a pound, they pushed me to my infant limits. And I found them entrancing. There's something about flatfish. Apart from on a plate, I'd never seen one before and I just loved the undulating, magic carpet way that they fought. Mind you, on my old bamboo rod that had as much give in it as a bedstead, sensitivity wasn't much of an issue.

All these decades on, I still enjoy fishing for flounders but today, I do so in a rather unusual way. I wait until the tide is well out and then I take a fly rod – a six-weight is fine – out onto the flats and look for the low water pools. This is where the flounder congregate at the lowest water and a small shrimp pattern – say a size eight or 10 – pulled slowly back along the sandy bottom brings the most surprising results. At first, you think you've hooked a ball of weed. And then the weed moves once again in that strange flapping up and down sort of motion. And another perfectly formed flounder slides to the hand. It's up to you whether you eat one for your supper.

But of course, a two-or three-pound flounder is a monster. A 200-pound halibut is about par for the course.

One of my bibles is *How to Catch Alaska's Trophy Sport Fish* by Christopher Batin, 1984. I can't think how many times I've read it, drooling over the photographs of Alaskan monsters. It's the halibut chapter, though, that takes some beating… "All too often, anglers will hook into this largest member of the flat fish family, the halibut, hoping for a quick tug-em-up battle and into the ice chest. They soon learn, however, that trophy halibut are not easily fought or landed. These fish, often called barn door halibut – the term that literally describes their size – require a boatful of luck, plenty of grunt, and lots of prayer just to muscle them off the bottom! Battles lasting up to several hours are not uncommon. Even if an angler is lucky enough to land one, his work is cut out for him back at the boat dock. There, big halibut must be off-loaded with an overhead crane and weighed on a scale with springs large enough to support a half ton pick-up!" Now, doesn't a leviathan like that deserve to make it into the 50 somewhere?

Or how about this photo caption… "This angler is proud of his 315-pound halibut. The battle from hook up to gaff lasted over an hour. The fish had to be despatched with a shot from a .38 pistol before it was boated." Most of my fish I land with a net rather than shoot with a gun!

Mr. Batin ends his riveting chapter on halibut by saying, "The excitement of catching big halibut is best summed up by the comments of an elderly woman who had just disembarked from a tour bus while we were unloading a day's catch of halibut. The woman shook her head as she gazed upon a 60 pounder waiting to be cleaned. After asking numerous questions about the fish and the fishing she returned to her husband, who was taking pictures of the boat dock. 'Elmer,' she said in an enlightened voice. 'We're going to cash in these sightseeing tickets and go halibut fishing.' From what I understand, the couple left with a 124 pounder and a promise to return the following year."

My one and only halibut outing was less successful – as you will find out from my diary!

HALIBUT FACTS

• Halibut are very much a fish of the north, of cold, deep water. They are nomadic and adult specimens frequently travel up to 2,000 miles during the course of a year. They're also found down to a depth of 600 astonishing fathoms. My research seem to suggest that the Pacific halibut can reach a staggering 800 pounds. Mr. Batin states a big fish for Alaska will be 400 pounds and at this weight will almost certainly be female, perhaps 40 years old.

July, 1996. Disko Bay, West Greenland. From John Bailey's Diary.

I find it hard to get my head round this place. Perhaps it's the eternal sunlight and the fact that it's hard to know whether you should be awake or whether you should be asleep. Now it's six o'clock in the evening but it could be just as easily six in the morning. Gazing out over Disko Bay and I'm possibly as moved by what I see as ever before in my life. The water streaming from the glaciers shifts its colors from silver through to pearl through to orange and finally to gold for no apparent reason whatsoever. The icebergs float past, stately as white frost-encrusted cathedrals. Mists arise like spirits and then float away. Everywhere you look, there are strange happenings, sights to me totally inexplicable.

JJ and I go out with an Inuit sealer come fisherman and his two sons. The plan is to fish for halibut in water so deep and so cold that it defies all imagination. We spend some time motoring out of Disko Bay, going north I think. The two boys see a seal in the distance, get into a kayak and paddle away into the blinding light to hunt it. Their father watches them through binoculars. He never takes his focus from them. Not for a second. Polar bears, you see. These great white killers can slide off an iceberg, swim a quarter or a half a mile subsurface and then come up under the boat, tip it and kill his sons. It's a terrifying prospect. JJ and I are anything but excited about our chances.

The boys give up on the seal. They return to the mother ship and we steam on to a place surrounded by bergs. Here, where the air is like a fridge, the father says we will find the halibut. JJ and I get into a small boat with the two boys and we move perhaps 100 yards away from the main ship. We're perking. Uptide rod, multiplier reel, 100 pound line and a huge silver hooked-up rod as bait. It's ridiculous. We sit like garden gnomes lifting our rods rhythmically up and down, up and down, up and down. We've probably got 600 feet of line out each and the boys keep telling us to let more go. We can't take this seriously. This isn't fishing like we know it. We're giggling. The boys aren't pleased with us you can tell.

My rod thumps over. There's no other word to describe it. Silence. Johnny and I look at each other. Look at the rod which is bending like a flimsy reed under the power of something enormous. Whatever it is sulks. I gain perhaps 20 feet of line. This is easy. We grin. Thumbs up. Now there are some heavy blows. The rod judders. Whatever I've got on and it feels huge, dives. The reel is grinding. It's furious. There's a wrench. It jams. I'm in danger of being pulled overboard. One of the boys leaps forward, knife in hand, the line is sliced. The rod leaps back and the most breathless two minutes of my life have come to an end.

We're back in the town and it's two in the morning. The party is just filling up. Gorgeous Danish girls are flocking in along with dark-haired Greenlanders. All I can do, though, is gabble about my lost butt and get slowly and sadly drunk on locally distilled vodka.

GREY MULLET *Chelon labrosus*

More Ghost Than Fish

Region: Mediterranean, Eastern Atlantic from Southern Scandinavia to North Africa

"If I don't catch a mullet soon, I'll shoot myself! That makes 81 tides fished this summer alone without a single, serious chance. I'm running out of ideas and inspiration. I sense this is beyond me, possibly beyond anybody. I'm seriously considering that these fish are uncatchable."

John Bailey's diary, August 1973.

Target weight: 6lbs
Dream weight: 10lbs
Areas: Mediterranean and eastern Atlantic.
Food: Algae

SUMMARY
These are fish of warm fertile waters. A major problem for the angler is that they are largely algae feeders, scrapping nutrition from the surface of the muds.

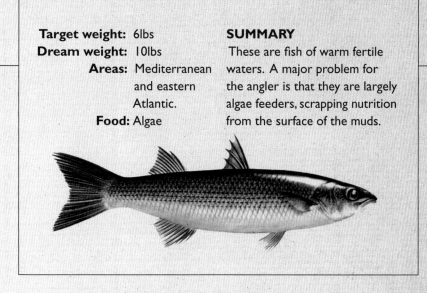

I didn't catch a mullet that year. I haven't caught many since. And that's why mullet are in the 50. They simply have to be the most elusive fish on the planet. But let me elaborate, there are mullet and there are mullet. I'm talking about creek mullet here, the fish that inhabit marshland, that follow the tides, whose habits are barely understood. On the other hand, there are harbour mullet. If you want to see these, go into the marinas along the Costa del Sol in Spain.

Marbella is probably your best bet. There in idyllic sunshine, you will see the yachts of the fabulously wealthy swinging at their moorings.

This is a place for the beautiful, the rich and mostly, the Russians! The cafés are a good place to hang around and watch the parade of women, Ferraris and all the glamour that surrounds these unlikely sailors. But, if you're an angler, it's the water itself that attracts the attention. Throw in a piece of your roll. If the seagulls don't get it, the mullet will. The marinas heave with them. There are mullet everywhere. Big, turquoise fish, always hungry, always scavenging. You'd have a netful in minutes if you were allowed to fish. But what would be the point? Where would be the satisfaction in that? No, give me the mullet of the wild marshes.

When the water was about knee deep, those 200 mullet reappeared. They found the net, they nosed it. They nudged it. Then, group after group, charged at it, leaping into the air and hurdling it by sometimes a clear two feet. All 200 fish escaped. Their triumph was complete.

It doesn't make things easier that this is a dangerous landscape. The mud in the creeks can be treacherous. There are areas of soft sand where it is possible to sink almost immediately to your waist. The tides themselves are unpredictable. Sometimes they come fast and sometimes they creep up behind you, blocking your escape route. Sometimes a mist comes down and in the deafening silence you get confused, totally lost and can easily wander out to sea. Men have died here. You simply don't take risks.

There are chinks of light. Rumour has it in Ireland, on beaches where a lot of kelp gets washed up, the rotting mass gets blown by flies and maggots are the result. At high tide, the mullet rummage in the kelp, find the maggots and become susceptible to these on a hook or even to small, white, artificial flies. And there have been stories coming from Anglesey which has similar areas of flooded salt marsh. There, it's said, anglers have caught mullet on tiny, black and brown Goldhead flies. It was these stories that gave me a second wind of inspiration...

My homeland of North Norfolk, England, is typical of the places that this type of mullet frequents. It's often hard to divide the land from the water and there is no clear distinction. What's land one minute is under water the next. The tides are forever slipping and sliding, filling creeks, swamping the headland, sliding across the salt marsh, bringing the mullet in from the open sea close by. It's fascinating to watch. The water is crystal clear and frequently the mullet will follow the tidal flow where it's only inches deep. You can see their fins, you can count their scales, you can look deep into their unblinking eye. You're so close, yet you're so far away.

I can't even begin to enumerate the different ideas I've pursued. Flies of all shapes and sizes. Spinners – large and small, often laced with red wool, scraps of ragworm or tipped with maggots. Bait fishing with bread, lugworm, lobworm, ragworm, sweetcorn, maggots, red worms, bread paste, cheese paste, bananas, peas, mixed meat, pasta, and even small balls of stiffened, harbour mud. I have pre-baited for weeks in the same cove. I've drifted bread down creek after creek. I've caught bass, flatfish, crabs, and even one small tope. But mullet, none.

It was in 1974 that I decided to net them. Nicky and I got to one of the best runs at low water and waited, sitting on the marsh, swapping stories. The tide swept in and with it came the mullet. 50, 100, perhaps 200 fish swept past us foraging up the creek. Then, we laid our net. It was large and secure, and we were confident. Again, we waited. The tide slowed, peaked and then, at last, began to ebb.

GREY MULLET FACTS

- Fishing for them? There's the rub! Since 2006 I've had increasing success. My tally now stands at a dozen or more. Brown Goldheads are better than black. Size 18s are better than 16s but 14s hold a big, running fish the most securely of them all. The key seems to be to work the fly slowly. If you don't disturb the fish then one in 50 will take.

June 2006, 4.00 a.m. Norfolk, England.

The light is growing all the time and it is a sensational time to be alone, in this completely unspoilt place. There is mist over the marsh but the sun soon disperses it. I arrive hot at the Watch House. It's a walk of perhaps half an hour and the shingle sucks at your feet. The tide is definitely on the flood. Far out in the main body of water, I see seals riding in the flow. They are hunting mullet, too. I'm waiting for the creek in front of me to fill. There's samphire, that wonderful, maritime asparagus in the margins and the mudflat is criss-crossed by wading birds. A barn owl flies noiselessly overhead.

Now, there's splashing 100 yards out. The mullet are on their way. They're driving themselves into water that barely covers their backs. The excitement as always is immense. I can't believe that I'm going to fail again.

And now they are here, 10 yards in front of me. The water is crystal, the sun is up, sight fishing is what this is all about. I guess there are 40, perhaps 50 fish now within casting range and some look big. The one out there, to the right, just has to be a 10 pounder. I'm using a five pound leader and, on the end, I have a size 16 black Goldhead nymph. My first casts spook fish each time. I learn to cast in water that has no mullet present and wait for the fish to appear. There are four, perhaps five fish now, within two feet of my fly. I twitch it so, so slowly. This must be my twentieth cast. And the fly is taken. It's so gentle. I could easily miss it. I half think I'm dreaming. But I tighten and there's a mullet hooked, a mullet just as bewildered as I am.

It's off. This is a scorching run. No bonefish is faster. The line and 20 yards of backing has gone in seconds. It's heading towards the sun. I can see it jump, black silhouetted over the glow. The line snaps. That's it. Gone. Heartbroken. So few chances. Lead in my boots. I walk homewards.

MARLIN *Makaira nigricans*

The Bull of the Sea
Region: Worldwide

"The seas soon ran mountainous and we had to turn in. On the way we sighted an enormous black marlin riding the swells. He rolled like a water-logged wreck. His length was tremendous, and the upper lobe of his tail, nearly three feet. I went quite out of my mind!

"We trolled a dead bait in front of the monster. Either it did not see it or refused to strike. But we tried again after following him a goodly way, during which time the sight of his color and breadth and length worked more havoc with me. If I had only had live bait! The second time he made at my dead kahawai and looked it over while I held my breath. But no! He did not like it and he went down for good."

Tales from a Fisherman's Log *by Zane Grey, compiled in 1927 and published in 1978.*

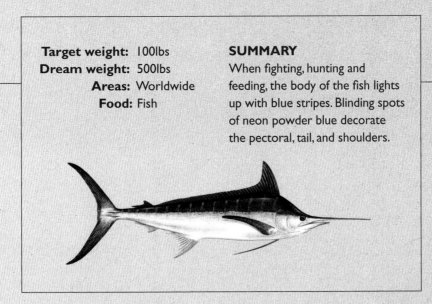

Target weight: 100lbs
Dream weight: 500lbs
Areas: Worldwide
Food: Fish

SUMMARY
When fighting, hunting and feeding, the body of the fish lights up with blue stripes. Blinding spots of neon powder blue decorate the pectoral, tail, and shoulders.

I realize this is not logical. A life is a life no matter how great or how small. A minnow should, therefore, be as precious as a marlin. The only difference in catching one rather than the other is in scale. That's what my head tells me but in my heart I don't quite believe it. Isn't there something about the marlin that makes them so incredibly special?

I'm influenced in this by my love of Hemingway and that little masterpiece, *The Old Man and the Sea*. Everybody has read it but perhaps it's rusty in your memory. Revisit it please. Witness afresh how the Old Man's respect for the fish grows as the epic battle continues through the long, wearisome hours. Think of the Old Man's pity for the giant fish pulling remorselessly through the seas. How the marlin is both wonderful and strange almost other-worldly in its power and steadfastness.

The Old Man begins to see marlin as fish apart, unnervingly special. He remembers meeting up with a pair of marlin and how the male fish always let the female fish feed first. The female was hooked. She made panic stricken despairing leaps and the male stayed with her throughout the battle. Only after the female was landed did the male leave her and then after a great leap so that he could see her body in the boat for the last time.

It's as though during that endlessly enduring battle, the Old Man and the marlin become as one. Remember how the Old Man whispers, "I'll stay with you until I am dead…fish. I love and respect you very much but I will kill you dead before this day ends." This is Hemingway's appreciation of that elemental bond between man and the unfathomable powers of nature.

Of course, as we all know, the saddest part of the tale begins after the leviathan is finally conquered, upon the endless, pitiless voyage home. Increasingly, the Old Man regrets having killed the fish, he regrets having gone so far from port. He regrets the impossibility of saving the dead marlin from the encircling sharks. As more and more of the marlin disappears down the throats of the predators, the Old Man's victory over the fish appears increasingly pyrrhic. By the time the Old Man makes it back to harbour, the carcase of the fish is totally destroyed, a capture made a complete waste of a fish for which he had so much love and respect. All the Old Man can think is, "I wish it had been a dream now and that I had never hooked the fish and was alone in bed on the newspapers."

So where do I stand when it comes to hunting the marlin? Should we be like the Old Man and dream that we never hook this most incredible of fish? Should the marlin be in the 50? There's one man to ask. Keith Elliott is sure of the reply.

MARLIN FACTS

• The blue marlin is probably the biggest of the bill fish and may exceed 15 feet in length. Weights of 2,000 pounds have been recorded. The black marlin runs it close; however, the striped marlin is somewhat smaller, rarely exceeding 13 feet and 600 pounds. The average weight is probably closer to 200. The white marlin are slightly smaller still.

March 2008. Keith Elliott in conversation with the author.

Of course marlin have to be included. I can't begin to describe how utterly thrilling it is to have something the size of a marlin on the end of a line. It's almost impossible to believe it. I've hooked a black marlin off Malaysia and when I saw it come out, leave the water, it was the great moment of my fishing life. It's almost impossible to believe that something so enormous can jump so high. It's a sight that defies nature, defeats your logic.

Of course, I know that fly fishing for creatures like this really is a nonsense. And I'm aware that trolling is a dull way of catching them. I also know that in many cases, money makes up for skill. But even taking all these things into account, there's just something so gripping about hunting marlin. Watching them approach. Watching them change color. The excitement of being close to a fish as phenomenal as these. The fire just never dies in you. You know I'm no great sailor and sometimes I look at a rough sea and take a great breath. I ask myself whether I want to go out but it's just something I have to do. It's a compulsion.

You talk about Hemingway and his Old Man. I think you've got it wrong. I don't think Hemingway ever meant at all that we shouldn't fish for marlin. He just wanted to emphasize that we have to respect them. It's a bit like his take on bull fighting. It's not necessarily something that's always easy to justify but it's an activity that's irresistible. A compulsion, if you like. And both the bull and the marlin are the supreme examples of creatures that nature can produce.

I agree with you, of course, we never want to witness again the sight of marlin hoisted by cranes on the boat docks. But we won't. The advent of circle hooks has helped. Catch and considerate release is now pretty well standard worldwide. Perhaps through the Old Man, the marlin is now accredited with what Hemingway always wanted. That's the love, the respect and the awe of the fishing world for his great fish.

SEA BASS *Dicentrarchus labrax*

Salt Water Sensations

Region: Atlantic coast of North America, Southern
Norway to Atlantic coast of North Africa

"Look for diving gulls. Look at the contours of the shore at the lowest of the tides, watching for features like gulleys, rough ground, kelp, depressions or incoming freshwater. Look out for fast water and anywhere the water is doing something unusual. Sandbars. Spits where the water is pushed into a back eddy. Kinks in the beach, perhaps. Don't neglect sea defenses groynes, freshwater streams, anywhere that food can collect. Look for the blue water – areas or channels where there is a good drop-off. You are putting together a jigsaw here, building the pieces, tracing the lifestyle of a truly wild species."

Justin Anwyl, bass guide.

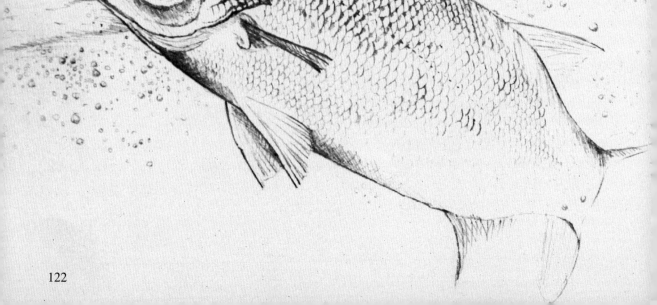

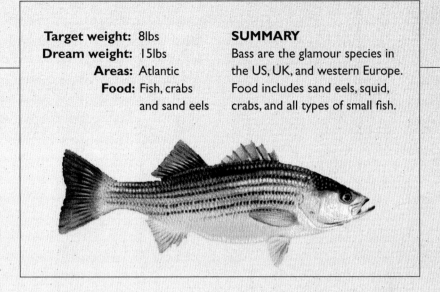

Target weight: 8lbs
Dream weight: 15lbs
Areas: Atlantic
Food: Fish, crabs and sand eels

SUMMARY
Bass are the glamour species in the US, UK, and western Europe. Food includes sand eels, squid, crabs, and all types of small fish.

It's the last sentence of Justin's introduction that holds the key. Tracing the lifestyle of a truly wild species. That's bass fishing. That's why bass are in the 50. That's why they have devotees both sides of the Atlantic and throughout the Mediterranean.

It was in 2000 that I spent morning after morning fishing for the huge American equivalent of the European bass, the striped bass, along the beaches of New York. I didn't catch one. I didn't hook one. But I saw them hunting from time to time and I talked to scores of New Yorkers who were in thrall to these fish. Most of them were fishing with bait like mullet, sand eels, squid, crabs, and clams but some guys were fishing, and I talked to one, with a fly rod. It's hard work, he admitted, but each year he claimed to catch fish of 20 and even 30 pounds on large streamer patterns pulled through the surf. He released them all, he said. It was just the most exciting thing he'd ever done. Considering he had been a test pilot and was working in corporate finance, it said a lot about the thrills of striped bass.

In 2004, I spent time with Juan Del Carmen fishing for European bass along the coast line of Andalucía in Spain. The beaches around Marbella were those he loved the most, and he'd wait until there was a good surf running and, as Justin Anwyl advises, he'd be looking for groynes, rocks, jetties, anywhere that food would collect. Juan often fished a popper. He'd drag it back fast, creating a churning wake. The bass would go mental. Sometimes they wouldn't take but chase the fly, harrying it, berserk with furious interest. Then he'd put a conventional, small fish or shrimp pattern to the bass and hook it every time. These were big fish. Sometimes they were 10 or 12 pounds in weight, and he'd be playing them in five foot of water, standing on tiptoe, coping with the surf, battling with a fish 50 yards off and still going strong. We'd only go and sit in a bar when we absolutely had to. When the light or bad weather hit and there was no way even Juan, the most dogged of all fishermen, could carry on. That's why I was surprised, one day, when he kept looking at his watch and finally pulled off at five in the afternoon. Was he losing his stomach for it, I wondered? "No way, man," he replied. "Just my first baby boy was born at two this afternoon and I should go and see him, but I'll be back. Babies are fine, but bass are the thing."

My best place? I love Wales, Devon, the Outer Hebrides, and Ireland for big fish but, being a Norfolk lad, give me that county's north coast any time. You're wading through the shallow surf, fly rod in hand, pursuing fish fresh in with the tide. Gulls whirl above you as you see the sea explode before you. On the retrieve, the fly is hammered and your six weight outfit is under violent attack for five pulsating minutes before a glinting, silver bass comes to your hand. There's little to beat the loneliness of the marshes, the creeks, the estuaries, and the deserted beaches while eating a fresh-grilled bass as the sun goes down.

SEA BASS FACTS

- A lot of anglers insist on all bass being returned and you can see why. They take five years to mature, making a 10 pounder a creature of iconic importance. In the UK at least, you must be aware of size limits. Typically, these are around 14 inches but they can vary from region to region. In the UK, the growth of bass numbers is down to the 40 or so designated bass nursery zones that are given protection from netting.

February, 2008. Ksar Massa Beach, south of Agadir, Morocco

It's a bass all right, not quite the sea bass of Europe but a spotted bass, a close cousin and it's gorgeous. Radouin is with us. This morning he took us to a bird sanctuary where we saw ibis, spoon bills, flamingo, black-winged stilts and Barbary partridges. Now, fly rod in hand, he's taken us to the beach and he wants us to eat the fish. He says we've got to grill it or steam it in a tagine. But Sarah is adamant. Too small she says. Back it goes. But what a fish. What a place. I don't think I've ever fished in such water. The sea here, the Atlantic, just comes surging in with a muscle and a relentlessness that's hard to comprehend. You stand in the desert two miles away and you still hear the sea. At night, it churns through your dreams. This is sea with attitude, with presence, with menace. It makes my homely North Sea seem like a puddle.

Radouin says that the trick is to find those gulleys which have rock beds to them rather than sand. You know when you've got it right because the fly, generally a rough orange shrimp pattern, just gets battered. The power of the take in this surf is hard to take in. The bigger fish come in June the locals are telling us. Sod that, says Sarah, these are big enough. When we're not catching the spotted bass, we're catching fish like bream or jacks of every shape and size. But they're nearly all this dramatic, metallic silver that we love.

This is the wildest saltwater fly fishing. Juan would be whooping with glee. My test pilot would be white-knuckled on the rod butt. Water cascades over us. It's thrilling and it's frightening. You can see the fish hit the fly through windows in the water. Shapes bullet out of nowhere. The rod slams, the waves boom, we're drenched, happy, drained. We feel pummelled by the ocean. It's exhausting stuff. You can only take so much.

There's a perfect sunset as Sarah washes the gear off for the day. We notice a desert fox sitting on its haunches 50 yards off, head cocked, watching us. I make a move for the camera and it's up, trotting its way into the shadows of the western Sahara.

BARRACUDA

Sphyraena barracuda

Fighters of the Salt

Region: Tropical and temperate oceans of the world

"We'll be hitting all sorts of guys around the reefs, and they'll batter you. I don't care if you're on fly or lure or bait. You just gotta hold 'em like they were a runaway bull. Let them dive, and you've lost them. Simple as that. I'll be checking knots. The gear's gotta be a hundred percent boys. You might only be into a fish of five pounds but by God if its a 'cuda, you'll think it's 50."

Top Florida Guide, Dave Gibson, in conversation with JB, May 2005.

Target weight: 15lbs
Dream weight: 30lbs
Areas: Warm oceans
Food: Fish

SUMMARY
A fish of the scorching first run. Can grow to 100lbs plus. Fiercely aggressive with ferocious teeth,

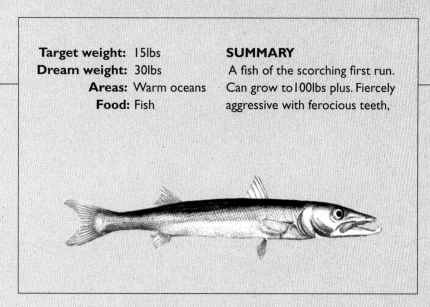

Barracuda are often overlooked by sport anglers in favor of more glamorous fish of the flats. But there is a lot going for big barracuda especially. These tend to come onto the flats when the weather turns cold and water temperature drops during January, February, and March, when bonefish and permit often sulk in deeper water.

Another bonus is that barracuda are happy to feed on the surface or just beneath, which makes for highly exciting top water fishing. Try poppers or long, thin flies dressed with a white belly to imitate 'cudas prime food sources, the needlefish.

I love 'cudas. They're just so mean, so lean, so munchy. Perhaps it's the pike angler in me. I remember off the Bahamas seeing a creature that MUST have been six feet long. I tell you, I was half scared to cast to it. My retrieve was so half-hearted the fish simply scoffed. I caught one later that probably weighed a fifth as much and that took me on a first run that simply scorched the reel.

Another reason I'm looking at 'cudas is because of Dave Lambert. Dave is another of these young adventurers that I'm so fortunate to mingle with. In fact, perhaps Dave is the wackiest of them all. Give him a whiff of adventure and he'll be off. It doesn't matter how far. It doesn't matter how unknown. That's where he'll be. I'm going to quote from one of the longest, most inspiring emails it's ever been my fortune to receive. Here's a guy that lives for his fishing and the people and environments the sport takes him to meet. Here's a guy at the sharp end of what we do.

BARRACUDA FACTS

• Barracudas are elongated fish with powerful jaws. The lower jaw of the large mouth juts out beyond the upper. Barracudas possess strong, fang-like teeth. These are unequal in size and set in sockets in the jaws on the roof of the mouth. The head is quite large, pointed, and it is pike-like in appearance.

24th March 2008. Dave Lambert's account of a trip to the Indian Ocean.

I had been living on a small island in the Indian Ocean for the previous nine days. There were maybe 20 bamboo beach huts and there was a good mix of young people from all around the world. Most were there for the yoga or the meditation, or simply to unwind. Max, an Austrian, was there for the fish. His girlfriend Katy was there for the sun.

We'd enjoyed two weeks excellent fishing by this point. Most of it was spinning or trolling and we had caught GTs, blue fin trevally, big eye trevally, grouper, green Job fish, king fish, black dollar, dog tooth tuna and I even, eventually, got my yellow fin tuna. Just holding that fish in my arms was emotional. So perfect. So beautiful. The best thing in the world except maybe after some of those Russian chicks

Anyway, Max had already landed a large barracuda the day before and to my surprise he said he was going diving leaving me with the boat to myself. Fishing alone is okay but I always get the largest amount of pleasure seeing people catch their first fish. Especially out there where everything fights so hard. So I invited a couple of Russian / Israeli guys to come out with me. The two Ds David and Dimitri they jumped at the chance. They'd been fascinated by what Max and I had been catching in the days before. And, amazingly, Katy decided to come, too. Seems Max wouldn't let her go out, he always said she was bad luck to any boat. And so, for a while, it seemed.

We went out in a local boat, a dungi, with two of the local guys that we'd been fishing with all week. Cha Cha the older of the two, was an absolute master of the seas.

He knew when and where fish would be each day and every state of tide. I owe virtually everything I caught on the trip to this man. If you ever read this, thank you mate.

I don't know if it was because of Katy but the fishing was slow by comparison with the previous days. Trolling around the edge of the reefs produced a few small but beautiful coral trout and I hooked and lost a good fish in the open water. Katy had showed little interest in actually fishing all day and I was trying hard to keep David and Dimitri focused but I felt their interest waning. I tried to explain to them how just one bite can transform a day into an unforgettable one and that that bite can come any second... fishermen know this but for non-anglers it's difficult to get around.

Anyway, Cha Cha signalled to me it was time to start heading back. We still had a good run because we'd come a long way out and surprisingly Katy decided at this late stage to take over a rod. It was then I knew that something would happen. Sitting side by side at the stern, I started talking about fishing, answering her questions, telling her how women often catch the largest fish of all. Think Miss Ballentyre.

Minutes passed and I knew that if a fish was coming it would have to be soon, as the strain of dragging a foot long Rapala at a rate of knots, with no rod rest or harness, was beginning to show on the girl. Then it happened. Though it was no surprise, it still came with a ferocity that shocked. That fish hit so hard and took line so furiously Katy was screaming and laughing simultaneously. I panicked, shouting instructions, falling over myself. But Cha Cha was rock calm. The speed of the fish was blistering. So often, because of slack line, I thought it had come off but it was simply overtaking the boat. And close by the boat it went absolutely mental. The line fizzed through the water. The reel simply screeched. The faces of my three students I can't begin to describe. Aghast. Agog. Amazed. Blown away.

GIANT TREVALLY
Caranx sexfasciat

Bruiser of a Fish

Region: Tropical Pacific & Indian Ocean waters

"Giant trevally, up to and over 100 pounds, haunt the passes, ready to take lures and give any anglers a beating. Anyone who lands one of these broad, dark shield-shaped fish over 80 pounds in weight knows he has been through a fight. Not only are they stubborn fighters, but many lines and leaders are cut as the trevally bore down in the deep water alongside the reefs. The ulua or saqa, as the giant trevally is called in Fiji, deserves rating with cobia, yellow tailed kingfish, and amber jack as the reef champions."

From Big Fish and Blue Water *Peter Goadby, 1970.*

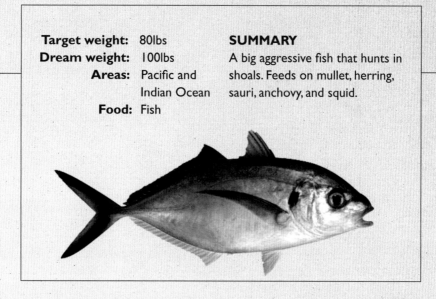

Target weight: 80lbs
Dream weight: 100lbs
Areas: Pacific and Indian Ocean
Food: Fish

SUMMARY
A big aggressive fish that hunts in shoals. Feeds on mullet, herring, sauri, anchovy, and squid.

The giant trevally. The GT. A bruiser of a fish. Henry Gilbey has said that they can't help themselves from hitting a lure or a fly. They're so furious to feed that nothing makes them afraid. They just have to attack everything within their horizons. That's how Akshay Malavi has described them to me as well. Fish that just go mental. I love Akshay and the spirit of the man. I met him years ago, fishing for mahseer in southern India, but it was obvious that giant trevally were figuring large with him even then.

"I've always, for the longest time, wanted to go to the Andaman Islands for the fish there, and especially for the giant trevally," he once said to me. "It's just been one of those places I've thought about a lot. I was lucky enough to meet a chap from there at a watering hole in Bangalore who ran a business exporting live grouper to Hong Kong. Suited me fine as all his fishing was done by hand line. About as close as you can get to rod and line in this country. A month later, Darran, a couple of friends and I had our tickets booked and headed off to

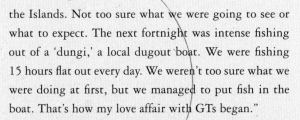

the Islands. Not too sure what we were going to see or what to expect. The next fortnight was intense fishing out of a 'dungi,' a local dugout boat. We were fishing 15 hours flat out every day. We weren't too sure what we were doing at first, but we managed to put fish in the boat. That's how my love affair with GTs began."

Fishing flat out hours on end out at sea under a blazing sun doesn't surprise me. Akshay lets nothing come between him and potential success. Take the River Cauvery. Night after night he'll fish on some of the wildest parts of the river oblivious to the dangers of elephant or leopard. He likes to target the narrower channels where he knows the mahseer will pass and he's not afraid to hook big ones, on his own, in the jet black of the Indian night. I love it when he comes back to the camp in the morning, his eyes alight, stories of the night streaming from his lips. He bubbles with that energy, that vibrancy, that passionate love for what he's doing.

GIANT TREVALLY FACTS

• The habitat of the giant trevally can range from estuaries to coral reef systems. You tend to find smaller fish prevalent in the estuaries and rivers. The larger trevallies move out to deeper water where there are reefs, drop-offs, and channels. They look for strong currents and a deeper water environment. Trevally will also venture onto flats, headlands and shallow water in their search for food. Reef edges are well worth exploring and points where pounding swells hit the reef.

A day in the Andaman Islands with Akshay Malavi.

I wake to the sound of birds on Havelock where we are based for a week of fishing for GT. I've already spent a couple of days out with a lone French client who was a keen fisherman and has spent many a week in fishing wild places in the tropics. It's his first trip to the Andaman Islands and he's spent the first few days of his trip fishing out of a dungi and has been reasonably successful. But the highlight of his days so far is a reasonable barracuda. A big one by any standards but I've seen bigger. Heading off to the harbor, I wonder how the day will be and what we'll manage to catch. We need a big fish. A big GT would be magnificent. I begin to pack our lunch and fruit into the cooler and I'm joined by the Frenchman already up and ready. Then my boat boys appear and over a quick breakfast and a couple of black coffees, we decide the areas we'll cover and how we'll go about fishing them.

What we specialize in, here in the Andamans, is 'popping', basically the use of a cup-faced floating surface lure that creates a large splash or 'pop' when retrieved in a series of jerks. Most clients visiting this part of the world are popping fanatics who have the sole aim of targeting the GTs. The Andaman waters teem with giant trevally along with species like grouper, coral trout, Job fish, red bass, dog tooth tuna and the occasional reef shark. Coffee over, we reach the jetty which is a buzz of activity as a ferry is about to arrive from Port Blair. Ferries are the lifeline in the Andaman Islands, transporting locals, tourists and rations. We load up the boat and head off towards the east as the ferry rounds the western corner of Havelock. We've got to catch some big GT on popper and see what else we can tempt with these floating lures. Conditions are perfect. A sunny day, with a light chop. Perfect for poppers. As we head up towards Inglis Island we looked for bait schools. Bait schools are a sure fire way of getting into GTs. The schools, you see, stay on top as the GT attack them from below. We keep our eyes peeled and notice a few schools but none look harassed, none provide us with any GTs. Inglis is a beautiful island that's not too far way and it's always been a good hunting ground for the trevally. Now conditions are even more perfect with the wind blowing from the northeast so that our drifts are all along the reef's edge.

On our first drift our poppers are smashed by GTs but we only manage to land one small one, a beautiful specimen all the same. The next two drifts provide us with nothing but a white bellied sea eagle that swoops to pick up our poppers repeatedly. An amazing and awe-inspiring bird.

We switch to plugs and repeat the drift. I feel a thump on my line like I've struck reef but in a flash my braid begins to pour off the reel. A large grouper heads straight back to his favourite hole in the reef. I put the brakes on him and bring him to a stop. I haul him up from the depths from which he came spitting bits of octopus in protest. A few photographs later we send the grouper back to his home in the reef where he truly belongs. We have a couple of coral trout in quick succession, one of which is a beautiful fish. A Maori perch follows, one of the first I've caught on lure, followed by an incredible red and yellow speckled coronation trout. It's an amazing drift and we're catching fish because we've moved down deep. Giving Inglis Island a friendly glance over my shoulder, I pointed the boat towards the south and head off to another island with yet another amazing reef. This place is my GT paradise!

TARPON
Megalops atlanticus

The Silver King

Region: Western Atlantic, Gulf of Mexico, Central America west coast, Carribean, and the coast of northwest Africa

"It was just a couple of weeks later than this in 1928 that Hemingway made one of his first sorties after tarpon around the islands west of Key West. He gathered his mob together. A lot of them had nicknames – Dos, Don Pico and the like and they went out with Captain Bra's charter boat. They anchored in the Marquesas Islands, swam, caught fish for dinner and next morning at dawn, took a breakfast of thick Cuban coffee, Cuban bread, avocados and smoked fish. Then for the tarpon. The silver kings. Waldo Peirce (Don Pico) took top spot with a massive 183-pound fish. Perhaps Hemingway had his nose put out of joint. Perhaps that's why, later, he was so dismissive of tarpon saying, 'catching them can lose all enchantment once you become familiar with the aerobatics of this spectacular, inedible and short-winded fish.' Hemingway didn't like to be bested at anything."

From John Bailey's fishing diary, Florida, 2005.

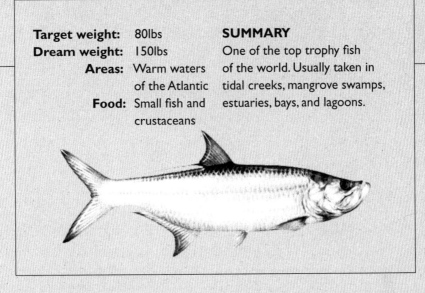

		SUMMARY
Target weight:	80lbs	One of the top trophy fish
Dream weight:	150lbs	of the world. Usually taken in
Areas:	Warm waters	tidal creeks, mangrove swamps,
	of the Atlantic	estuaries, bays, and lagoons.
Food:	Small fish and	
	crustaceans	

It was late April that year that John Wolstenholme, Howard Croston, Andy Murray, and I set out for a photo shoot, deep south in the Keys, the heartland of Hemingway's tarpon activities. We were guided by legendary Dave Gibson who stirred us all up with tales of massive fish, massive battles, massive triumphs. It was a period of high excitement and Dave certainly knew how to stoke our ambitions. We didn't have an easy time of it though. The weather was continually against us. Luck never went out way. We were so close but never, it seemed, close enough. I remember one evening fishing bait beneath the ruins of the old railway bridge that collapsed in storms with great loss of life in 1935. Winds of 250 miles an hour battered the structure and hundreds of war veterans who had been working on it were drowned. Hemingway was aghast that the authorities hadn't thought to evacuate them: brutal though his writing could be, he was strongly streaked with compassion. Odd that night, to think of the horrors 70 years before. I felt unlucky when a big silver fish – a tarpon of perhaps 80 pounds – swirled at my dead bait and refused it. At least I lived to tell my tale.

Our daily woes were increased by the girl in the diner where we ate each night. She was gorgeous. She had a boyfriend with whom she went out after tarpon, throughout the dark hours until dawn broke. She'd tell us of the 80 and 90 pounders they were catching. The spectacular fights under the starlit skies. The massive silver fish gleaming under the moon. She chuckled at our tales of woe. Hemingway would have loved her as completely as he would have despised us.

But as I said, we came close. On April 25th, Dave took us far away from the normal haunts into a shallow, secluded bay. We anchored for a while and watched the shore 100 yards away where mangrove roots writhed. It was hot and clear with little wind. Dave pointed. There they were. Groups of tarpon easing their way past.

Dave got Howard in close and, my God, was he in the zone! For an hour, it was Howard and those tarpon

and you didn't dare blink in case you missed the action. Follows. Refusals. A fish pricked and the dazzling sight of a massive hooked fish cartwheeling momentarily in the sun. Thrills laced with heartbreak. Better was to come.

TARPON FACTS

The tarpon of the warm coastal waters of the Atlantic Ocean have a lung-like swim bladder and well developed gills. You will find that in a well-aerated aquarium, young tarpon tend to die if they can't gulp air from the surface of the tank. This is probably explained because in nature young tarpon grow up in shallow, oxygen-starved waters of lagoons, mangrove swamps, mudflats and estuaries. If the oxygen content of the water is low, even adult fish will take it from the surface.

April, 2005. Florida Keys.

Dave wakes us up very early. We're in the boat and away long before the sky is light. We're heading ocean side and we've a long journey ahead. We pass settlements here and there, most sleeping, occasional lights flicking on. There are no other boats on the water. An occasional car's headlights picked out in the distance.

But we're here. Dave cuts the engine and we drift slowly towards an island emerging from the right. Dave understands the water here, tells us the tide is slowly moving beneath us, pushing the night's death toll of small fish and crabs along the tarpon highway, their number one feeding lane. He's right. The water is oily, thick with corpses and the big fish are here to feast. They're everywhere. You can see them rolling, close to us, unafraid. It's like their eyes are looking at us as these monstrous fish pass by. There's one so close I could reach out and touch it, letting my hand slide across its finely etched scales.

An atmosphere that tingles. Adrenaline washes over us in waves. Murray has a huge fish follow in a big silver fly. The bow wave grows as it nears the boat. The mouth opens and closes and the fish swirls away at the very last. This is fishing at the very limit of your mental endurance. This is the hyper excitement that Hemingway lived for.

I have a pull on a dead fish free-lined in the current and the reel screams endlessly. But it's a big jack. I'm not complaining. Deep down I'm disappointed. As the light grows, two things happen. Firstly, the tarpon drift away, satiated with food. Second, a massive electrical storm flickering on the horizon closes in upon us. This is dangerous, and soon we're sheering back through waterfalls of rain. Nothing else to do but hit Key West. Ten hours in Sloppy Joe's. Only margaritas quell the pain of that oh-so-nearly morning. Hemingway would love us now. Some of us get drunk. A couple of us pull girls. We get into a fight in the early hours. To be thrown out of Sloppy Joe's? Could be Ernest's twin.

BONEFISH
Albula vulpes

Lightening Quick

Region: Tropical waters worldwide

"Sitting in a bar in Nassau now. Looking back over the last 10 days it all seems very unreal. Sometimes after a trip, good to be alone, to digest what's happened. Still can't get over the speed of bonefish. I'd thought it was all rubbish that you had to let a four pound fish run 100 yards. Seven-weight outfit. Ten-pound tippet. I'd expected to stop an eight pounder in 20 yards. That first fish I just hung on. Bang. Elvis was furious. 'Those things swim at 26 miles an hour, man!' he screamed. 'Let them run or else. You know what "or else" means now. Don't be doing it no more.' Weird times. Weird fish."

From John Bailey's fishing diary. Nassau, 24th March 1999.

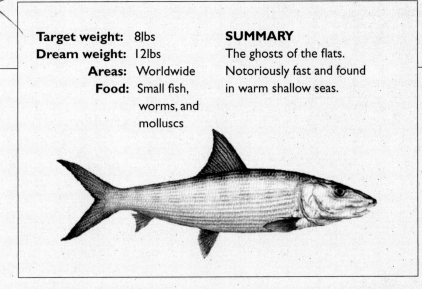

Target weight: 8lbs
Dream weight: 12lbs
Areas: Worldwide
Food: Small fish, worms, and molluscs

SUMMARY
The ghosts of the flats. Notoriously fast and found in warm shallow seas.

I'll be honest. Bones get into the 50 because I know there'd be an outcry if they weren't there somewhere. And of course, they do swim lightning quick. No denying that. If you detect my hesistancy it is only because of this. I've only had a couple of trips after bonefish and, in truth, I don't really understand them. I appreciate their agility, their sleekness, and the quite wondrous places on the planet they inhabit. I quite admit that watching a patch of agitated, "nervous water" coming towards you is thrilling in the extreme.

It's mesmerising, too, watching bones "finning" in the shallow waters of a mangrove swamp.

I understand a little what the bonefish game is all about...that you've got to look for deeper channels, depressions on the flat, bare patches amongst the turtle grass. I've begun to realize that bones change their coloration, their entire look. They're white over marl, and they sparkle like shards of glass over that turtle grass. It's something to do with those thousands of tiny, mirror scales that paint them with eternal camouflage.

I know, too, that bone fishing is all to do with reading the tide, the wind, and the supplies of food available. Probably the phase of the moon has got something to do with it, too. Like the very best of fish, bones have this mystery and magic about them. It's just that I haven't really, yet, been let into the secret.

My first bone fishing expedition was to Aklins Island at the bottom of the Bahaman chain. Fidel and Elvis were my principal guides and I wouldn't count the trip truly as a success. The weather was frequently sullen. So was Fidel. He somehow sensed that I wasn't in the zone and for that I could go to hell. The couple of times that he did spark into life were galvanizing. He was a man electrified. I was

blown away. His grace in the water was extraordinary. His control of tackle, his reading of the situation, his empathy with the fish all resonated with me. There's no doubt I was watching a master. But then, Fidel would switch off. He'd leave me on my own floundering and quite evidently not care a jot.

I disturbed fish badly on the vast flat known as Copper Bottom. I don't know if it was my footfall or my casting or whether the bones just didn't like the look of my face but they fled, and Fidel snorted. I didn't do any better in Lovely Bay where bones were finning over the bleached white sand. Fidel did well there. Yet again, I messed up. Probably got too close to them. I didn't get nearly as close as Fidel though and he got away with it. Once again, I was doing something wrong, something I couldn't decipher, something Fidel couldn't be bothered to explain to me. Fishing to me is all about the "brotherhood of the angle." It might sound quaint but it's important to me. If I'm fishing with someone, then it's like family blood flows in both our veins. It's not always the case, of course, I've fished with some total jerks who probably haven't thought that highly of me! Fidel wasn't a jerk, I don't think he thought me a total jerk either. It was more like he had his secrets and they were hard won and I'd have to work things out for myself.

I did better on an unnamed island that Elvis took me to one steaming, shimmering afternoon.

BONEFISH FACTS

• Bonefish very rarely stop swimming and are nearly always moving against the tide. They will climb onto a flat with the rising water and will work higher and higher as the tide continues to flood. As the tide falls, they drop back with it into deeper water – always looking for food. When a bonefish picks up food, you will find it blows water through its gills. You might see small patches of clouded water as a result. These puffs are very rapidly dissipated but are one of the clues to location.

March 1999. Island somewhere off Aklins.

Elvis has a plan. He's not communicating it to me but he's resolute. We've been in the boat 30 minutes, full steam ahead, never pausing, never looking anywhere but directly south. Now we come to a long, long sand spit. Perhaps you could call it an island even and he knocks back on the speed and we drift slowly onto the shore. It's a wonderful place. There isn't a sign of a footstep. It's like the place was created for the two of us alone. I guess the spit is some 50 yards across and, on the far side, there's a big, shallow bay. There are bones far out, finning. But they are a long way off and I doubt my ability to lay a fly gently at that range. The way Elvis is looking at me, so does he. So I wander off on my own. I'm not too bothered to be honest. It's brilliant here. A barracuda,

perhaps a meter long swims five yards out, almost following me step for step. I come to a huddle of small, windblown bushes and settle beside them. It's perfect peace. Now, 10 yards to my right I see two huge bonefish coming towards me. They're no more than inches from the shoreline. Their backs are exposed. They're feeding obviously. They haven't got a care in the world.

I shuffle back in amongst the bushes, perhaps four or five yards from the water's edge. I unhook the fly from the keeper ring. It's a tiny crab pattern. I ever so gently cast it out so that it's a foot from the bank in front of me. Then I pull it back in so that it's six inches, no more, from the dry sand. There's hardly any leader in the water and most of it, along with two yards of fly line, is lying on the beach. I'm not sure that this is in the rules, if it's pucker bone fishing, but my heart's beating like a drum and I certainly don't care.

It takes four minutes for the ambling fish to get close. Now they're inches away. I can see every scale, every fin ray. I twitch the crab ever so minutely and both fish bullet towards it. There's a blur. The reel's screaming. There's a bow wave reaching out to the horizon.

Elvis has seen it all. Now, hours later he's recounting it over dinner. I can see Fidel is weighing it up. He doesn't know whether to be impressed or deprecating. Was it a bit of inspired fishing or a sneaky bit of cheating? His decision hangs in the balance. He decides. "Cool man," he says. A nine pound bone, I know now, richly deserved.

COD
Gadus morhua

The World's Favorite Saltwater Fish

Region: North Atlantic

"A true surf caster is a man who loves the sea. Far beyond the prize of any fish he might land is the exhilaration of the waves. In the summer along the New Jersey coast they came in in sets of three, in great racing combers. You could hear their dull booms far inland. Then there was the smell of the salt marsh. When the wind was offshore, these arching seahorses raced in with long white manes streaming from their tips. From the marsh at sunset you heard the cry of shore fowl. The haunting, space hinting cry of the curlew; is there a more moving call by any sea? There were days of dull mist which blurred the headlands. Then a white fog, with the hot sun behind it, when the hissing surf shone like burnished silver."

From Going Fishing, *Negley Farson, 1942.*

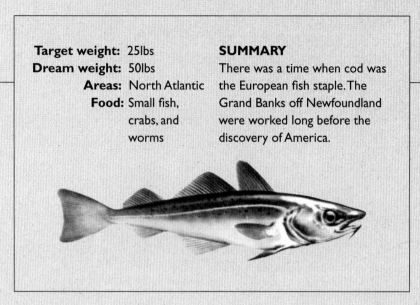

Target weight: 25lbs
Dream weight: 50lbs
Areas: North Atlantic
Food: Small fish, crabs, and worms

SUMMARY
There was a time when cod was the European fish staple. The Grand Banks off Newfoundland were worked long before the discovery of America.

No writer has ever examined the true nature of angling more sensitively. Farson says everything that we need to know about the true surf caster here – the cod fisherman of this present chapter. Cod fishermen are passionate about the sea, and they understand it completely, and if you want to catch a cod today, so great is the depletion in their numbers, a depth of knowledge is essential.

Years back, I met up with Tony Anderson, the type of man that Farson was describing. Tony was from the northeast of England, where life is rugged, where winter cod fishing from the beach is hard. He was a tall, gaunt man, tremendously strong for his late middle age. The day I was with him, he galloped across the rocks, I struggled in his wake. It was winter, freezing cold, the wind biting but the conditions were easy by comparison with what Tony had known and fished through during his life.

Fishermen are like any sportsmen. You look at them and you know instantly whether they are good, bad, or indifferent. From that first cast of his, I knew instinctively that Tony was very, very good. His gear and his clothing were not the smartest, but cod fishing on the northeast coast isn't a fashion parade. With the north wind belting onto that exposed coastline and the surf as high as a house, the last thing on anyone's mind was whether a jacket looked chic or not. Tony's gear that day could have been considered crude. A battered rod. A multiplier reel that had seen endless work. Thick line. Big hook. Massive weight. But in Tony's hands, you could see everything was made for the job.

Tony knew his patch well. He pointed out the best rock

coast and it was the hardest job I've ever known. Up way before dawn, walking miles out on the muds, chasing the receding tide. Back-breaking digging in the syrupy, clinging soil for lugworms often seven or eight inches long. The long walk back, spine creaking like a sailing ship, hands chapped and scarred and smarting in the salt. A wonderful life of freedom and open air and banter with mates, but a life gone now, redundant with the passing of the cod. Then, the demand for lugworm was endless. The piers and the beaches were full winter long with cod fishermen. Our worms went to the long liners offshore, men reaping harvests of cod. Once the first winds of winter blew, cod dominated our world.

spits, places where the bottom was sand, gravel, stone, or weed. He told me how he could predict the tides and use the currents to their maximum advantage. He knew exactly where to hammer his bait 80 yards out into the surf. Though it was daylight when I was with him, I knew he would have been just as accomplished in the night, when the wind was shrieking.

There was nothing hit or miss about Tony's style. He prepared his bait and I was impressed. His cocktails of crab and lug took him minutes to whip together. They were balls of juices and cod appeal. And when he hooked a cod, I was part of the excitement. The rod, that broom handle of a thing, slammed around. For several minutes he fought the fish against the undertow before, finally, he lost it in a far out crevice. It was breathless, hectic stuff but his footing was sure on the soaked, glass-like rocks. At the end of it all, Tony said it was a small fish, perhaps five pounds and there would be bigger to follow.

That's why cod are in the 50. For centuries, they've been the world's favorite saltwater fish. Fishing for them, from the shore, in the winter at night, is one of the hugely exciting forms of fishing. There's the fish itself. A big one. Creamy white and caramel browns. A fish that pulsates with vigour when it lies in the light of a Tillie lamp.

My own cod fishing took place in the winter of 1973/74. I was a worm digger then on the North Norfolk

COD FACTS

• With luck a cod can live for 40 years. The older they become the larger and more fertile they are. Bigger ones, obviously, attract better prices, too. However, such has been the over fishing of the North Sea that 90 percent of the cod present today are less than two years old. One cod in 200 is more than five years old. The cod population, therefore, is, almost without exception, too immature to maintain itself.

January, 1974. From John Bailey's fishing diary.

As usual, there's the endless discussion about which beach to go to. Billy wants this, Joe wants that and I don't think it matters a damn. There's cod everywhere at the moment. Big fish. We've dug our worms, we've got our gear, the van's ready, just let's get fishing lads. We choose, in the end, Runton. A nice beach. I like it. There's a big wind coming in and there'll be a lot of tide. The current will be massive and there'll be spray. I love it like this. I'm right. We get the Tilleys going, bait the hooks and hammer them out into the screaming night sea. It's brilliant. The rods are battered and we have to shout to hear ourselves above the gale. Ten o'clock. Eleven o'clock. Nearing midnight. Joe's saying we've got to be up in five hours and he's looking at his watch when Billy's rod clatters onto the shingle and is half pulled into the sea. I grab it and strike into something that hits back like a sledgehammer. I'm half dragged in, sea over my thigh boots. Billy takes over. "It's a cracker!" we're shouting. It's even taking line though he's pumping like crazy. Crazy. Crazy, crazy stuff.

It's a big one no doubt. It's nearly 10 past midnight when we get it, though we nearly lose it in the big waves. Yes. We're all laughing. Billy reckons 20 pounds and Joe says 15. We'll cut it into three halves shouts Billy, as happy as I've ever seen him. I've just got in. It's half past one. I'll set the alarm now for four. Shattered, exhilarated, I fall into sleep.

MACKEREL *Scomber scombrus*

Little Scorchers

Region: Throughout the world

"The sea trout fishing was just horrendous and the salmon was even worse. The water was dead low, hot, clear and we'd had so little rain the river was hardly moving. Just those times a guide absolutely hates. You get up in the morning knowing everything is against you and the chances of seeing a fish are next to none. Anyway, I have this guy who's desperate for a bit of action, any action. I say to him our only chance is down on the bay where we might pick up a mackerel or two. He's not convinced. But the thought of putting a bend in his rod cheers him up and he says we'll go for it. When we get there, the guy insists on using three small fish patterns on his leader. I try and tell him three is two too many. He's not having it. Mackerel are only two pounds at the most he says. I beg him. He won't listen. Within 10 minutes the inevitable happens and he hooks up three fish at once. The rod ends up like matchsticks. He's on the point of blaming me but then, thank God, he realizes that he's the one in the wrong. That's the way of it. These salmon and sea trout boys think they know everything. Until you've felt the power of a mackerel on a five-weight you know nothing at all."

Colin, guide at Inver Lodge, Connemara in conversation with the author in 2002.

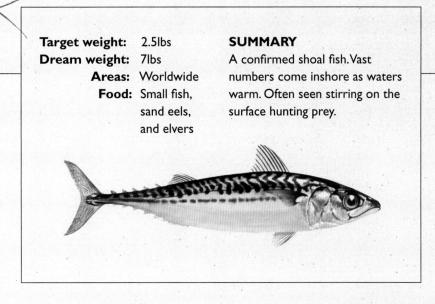

Target weight: 2.5lbs
Dream weight: 7lbs
Areas: Worldwide
Food: Small fish, sand eels, and elvers

SUMMARY

A confirmed shoal fish. Vast numbers come inshore as waters warm. Often seen stirring on the surface hunting prey.

Mackerel swim just about the world over in one shape or form or another. There are over 40 species, which include goliaths like the tuna, the bonito, and the wahoo. Here, though, we're lowering our sights but not in any way our aspirations. There are some dramatic mackerel of the smaller type. It was 2000 and I was spinning off the coast of Andalucía when my Mepps was hit by a hurricane. I'd been playing barbel for the week previously but I hadn't sniffed a fish that moved as fast. Mental. How a fish runs to all four points of the compass at once defeats me. When I got it in, it weighed five pounds. I thought I'd be looking at 50. I'm not exactly sure to this day what I caught. A mackerel all right but whether it was an Atlantic, Spanish, or a cero I've no clue. That's the bliss of fish. Half the time, especially when fishing the seas, you're only half sure of what you are catching.

I once saw a king mackerel caught in the Caribbean. I guess it weighed 20 pounds, and it looked like it was going to run for 20 miles. According to the books, king mackerel of nearly 100 pounds have been netted commercially. One hundred pounds. Beggars belief. I can't imagine the gear you'd need to land a fish like that.

Many members of the mackerel family have the ability to ship their pectoral, pelvic, and first dorsal fins into slots in their body. This makes them more streamlined and vastly increases their speed. As if it needed increasing in the first place. Records suggest that the blue fin tuna, the granddaddy of the family, can notch up swimming speeds of over 60 miles an hour. If you weigh over 1,000 pounds and you're hurtling through the ocean at that speed, you take some stopping.

So how come my Atlantic mackerel that are lucky to make three pounds in weight, get so easily into the 50? To a degree, this is a "be fair to fish" book! I always try to make anglers appreciate fish afresh because they're all so magical. And Atlantic mackerel have suffered hugely over the years from being hoisted aboard, hooked on feathers and ludicrously heavy gear. Even a blue fin tuna wouldn't fight long and hard against a crane and steel cable. Fish for them on equal terms, and an Atlantic mackerel is as electrifying as they come.

MACKEREL FACTS

• Mackerel of all species are obliging. They can be caught on feathers, on spinners, or on bait — shrimps and strips of any bait fish are killers. Surface-working plugs are fun. But, for me, give me the fly. When you find mackerel, then you'll catch them and you might just as well catch them the most fun way of all.

July, 2005. A beach a quarter of a mile from JB's house.

Evening after evening I've strolled down to the sea just to look. When mackerel are about in big numbers there's often surface evidence. But I've seen nothing. The few guys scattered along the beach have reported nothing either. I'm on the point of giving up. But it's become a habit this, this walk across the marshes, looking out for the barn owl I've become familiar with and the two herons that fish nightly by the dykes. I've a suspicion there's a bittern in the furthest reed beds but perhaps that's just too much to ask.

Anyway, it's a Thursday, the day's been hot and the wind, such as it's been, has blown offshore. There's small tide but it's coming in so, putting all the pieces of the jigsaw together, I'm confident. No, wrong word. Merely hopeful.

The spur of the shingle bank gives me a good view of at least a mile of seashore. My binoculars are, as ever, around my neck. There's excitement 200 yards to my left. The surface of the sea calm as a mirror, is puckered as though rain is falling hard. Waves of tiny silver fish are flickering on the surface. Whitebait. Whitebait only yards out, swarming in terror. Why on earth haven't I got my gear? I sprint back to my house. The fly rod, ready made up, is standing in the hallway. Pell-mell, I charge down the track, across the coast road, through the marsh to the sea. Everything is as electric as when I left it. I hammer out my fly and retrieve once, twice and I'm hit with a bang.

I'm never going to be pulled in or broken, but life feels frantic for the next five minutes. Can you believe this fish is only a pound and a half? I catch two. If I want, I could catch 22 but I take my brace back to my house, gut them and grill them and eat them out on the terrace, as overgrown as all fishermen's are, as the sun finally disappears.

This is good. This is as good as it gets and it's why I bought this cottage by the sea. It's why I long for summer evenings, southerly winds and the sunsets that light the sky 'til near midnight.

BLUE FIN TUNA *Thunnus thynnus*

The Greatest of the Greats

Region: North Atlantic, Pacific, and Indian Oceans

The weeks that followed were largely devoted to the capture of big fish.
Some of the records may be of interest:

Sand-shark (on rod and line) 620 lbs.
Hammer-head shark (on hand lines and 14 pound hooks)
1350 lbs. 17 ft. 6 in. long
Tiger-shark (on hand lines and 14 pound hooks) 1760 lbs. 20 ft. 9 in. long
Male swordfish (on hand lines and 14 pound hooks) 4500 lbs. 29 ft. long
Female swordfish (on hand lines and 14 pound hooks) 5700 lbs. 31 ft. long

From Unknown Tribes, Uncharted Sea *Lady Richmond Brown, 1924.*

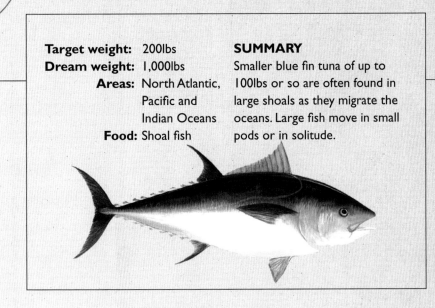

Target weight: 200lbs
Dream weight: 1,000lbs
Areas: North Atlantic, Pacific and Indian Oceans
Food: Shoal fish

SUMMARY
Smaller blue fin tuna of up to 100lbs or so are often found in large shoals as they migrate the oceans. Large fish move in small pods or in solitude.

The tuna, the tunny of legend is for me the greatest of the monster sea fish, but others push it to the limits of the 50. In the post Great War years, Lady Richmond Brown accompanied her friend Mitchell Hedges around the world, seeking out undiscovered tribes, phenomena of natural history, and especially, catching enormous fish. Mitchell Hedges book *Battles of Giant Fish* is a classic of its kind. Nothing was too big for Mitchell Hedges. He would use hooks I would have trouble in lifting. When his lines broke, he simply attached these hooks to chains! He wasn't averse, either, to using a 200-pound lump of sawn up shark as bait. Many years ago, an old man told me that he had been an acquaintance of both Richmond Brown and

Mitchell Hedges, and he pooh-poohed a lot of what they had to say. I don't know.

A lot of the photographs in *Battles* are pretty impressive. If he told a good story, it doesn't necessarily mean Mitchell Hedges was a liar. When you're after monsters, you can't be without a certain amount of gung-ho and a real dash of derring-do.

I'm thinking of guys like Henry Gilbey, tackling sharks on the west coast of Africa with just beach gear in water just a few feet deep. Looking at Henry's photographs, you think this isn't fishing. It's wrestling. But the prize for big fish adventure, in this book, must go to a one-time friend of mine, the legendary stalker, Chris Bennett.

Back in the 1990s Chris surmised that massive porbeagles might be found following the Gulf Stream, close to the north coast of Scotland. It seems that skippers had told him of sightings of big fish in nets, and any whiff of adventure was enough to have Chris totally focused. He hired a skipper, a crew, and a boat. He went out day after day, often in some of the worst of the weather that northern Scotland can conjure up. His phone calls to me during that period were a mixture of heroism and lunacy. Hour upon hour of being thrown round the decks of the storm-tossed ship. Freezing rain. Howling winds. As yet, not a sniff of a chance.

But, inevitably, knowing Chris, one morning came the call that I'd been hoping for. He'd caught his monster. I forget how many hundred pounds it weighed, but it was over five. It had fought him the short afternoon long, into the twilight and beyond. I forget how many miles they'd had to follow that massive shark, but it was several. At the end, he said, the fish was exhausted, and he was nearly dead.

A long while ago, tucked up in bed, my grandmother would tell me stories of equal power and passion. It seems that she and my late grandfather had spent at least three summers in the 1930s pursuing tunny (blue fin tuna) in the North Sea. She spoke of massive reels and rods you could poke an elephant with. Days at sea hunting down these enormous fish, weighing up to 1,000 pounds, as they hunted the large shoals of herring. Huge fish that sounded hundreds of feet beneath the boat. Monsters lashed high to the mast and brought back to the cheering crowds waiting in port. Great stuff. The sort of material that forged me into a fisherman, that made me feel that, somehow, I have a bond with the tunny. In 2002, I had a conversation, which follows, with a skipper going out of Donegal.

TUNA FACTS

• The blue fin tuna – or tunny – is the traveler of the oceans. It is built for power and for movement. Let's consider the muscle blocks that lie on either side of the backbone which help propel any fish. The weight of the muscle blocks in a goldfish is about 40 percent of the total fish. In a more active fish like the trout the percentage is stepped up to 65 or so percent. Nearly 75 percent of the entire weight of a tuna is given over to these massive, hard-working muscles.

<u>Derek Noble, an expert on tuna fishing in Ireland, in conversation with the author, 2002.</u>

Yes, John, what you're hearing is true. We might not have as many tunny as there were 80 years ago off your east coast but there's something special going on here right enough. A lot of it has got to do with the north Atlantic Drift I guess. It warms the coastal waters as they brush the west coast of Ireland. It's like a magnet to the tunny and they're following their prey close in to the coast of Donegal. If you're thinking of coming, mid August is perhaps the best time and you're talking big fish 400 pounders for sure but perhaps 500, anything up to 1,000 is possible.

Yes. It's heavy gear stuff. A 130 pound test with 16|0 hooks. Three hundred. Even 400 pound traces. The fish battle brutally. They pick up mackerel baits with a screaming run and they go long and hard, always pushing deeper. They don't tail walk but that doesn't detract, they are fish that just won't give in.

You don't want stormy weather for your sake or for the fishing. Given reasonable conditions you will find these massive fish close in, certainly within four or five miles of the shore. The mackerel are the key. Find them and you could find the tuna. You're never sure at what level the mackerel are running and where the tuna will be feeding but there are times, and this is amazing, John, when you will actually see the tuna hit into shoals of mackerel on the surface. And that's a sight, I'm telling you. There's no shortage of fish right now. Some of the groups are only five or six strong but 30 or 40 is probably more common. Just occasionally, there'll be hundreds, an area the size of a football pitch erupting with immense fish. In September last year I saw a colossal tunny come out of the water just 70 yards from my boat. It was over 400 pounds. Well over. Even the sea birds sheer off the surface as the fish plough through the waves at them. It's breathtaking whether you get a hook up or you don't.

The fish we've had go back of course. This is all in its infancy. There's no telling what the future is going to hold but we don't want in anyway to jeopardize it.

CHAPTER 3
GAME FISHING

ALLIS SHAD *Alosa Alosa*

Does Allis Live Here Anymore?

Region: Western Europe

"Today, I saw a quite remarkable fish over a period of perhaps 10 minutes. It was large – certainly five or six pounds. It seemed to be exceptionally narrow across the shoulders. But, interestingly, when it turned, it looked quite deep in the body though. The coloring was a liquid mix of silver along with a definite turquoise sheen to its upper flanks. The fish looked very graceful in the water. It was evidently restless, eager to get somewhere or do something. Perhaps it saw me. Perhaps it was following its own wishes but, soon, it disappeared off into the main river and was gone."

From John Bailey's fishing diary. May 31st River Wye, 1984.

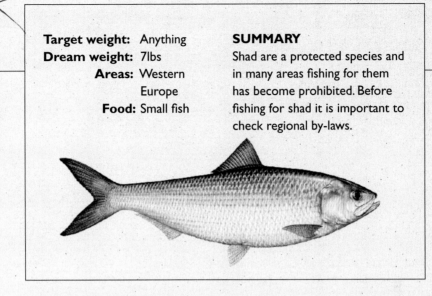

Target weight:	Anything
Dream weight:	7lbs
Areas:	Western Europe
Food:	Small fish

SUMMARY
Shad are a protected species and in many areas fishing for them has become prohibited. Before fishing for shad it is important to check regional by-laws.

Shad sneak into the 50 because of an element of mystery. Perhaps that's not fair. Any fish that resembles a tarpon, albeit a small one, has to be good. To catch any tarpon-looking creature on a four weight is not to be sneezed at. Add the fact that the country name, certainly in the UK, of the shad is the May fish and things get better. Hunting the shad is the perfect excuse to hit the river, fly rod in hand, at perhaps the best, freshest time of the year. May time and everything's singing shad.

And now we come to the mystery. What we're generally catching on the few remaining rivers that have a shad run, is the Twaite shad. There's nothing wrong with the Twaite. I've learned to love them. They average perhaps a pound and a half. I've probably had the occasional Twaite that's nudged three pounds on a generous set of scales. Size isn't really the issue though. They're game, they're beautiful, and it's a privilege to cast a line for them.

The presence of Twaite shad in the 21st century isn't anything like it once was. A few centuries ago, they flocked up many of our rivers. Now, sadly, they run the Severn and the Wye notably. The Shannon gets some fish. There are probably other rivers that see a few. Certainly the Loire has its fair share. You don't wander down to any river in May with fly rod in hand and expect to catch one. Not now. The Twaite's a fine fellow and you treat him with respect.

But the Twaite has a close relative, the Allis. And here's the mystery. It's a pun I've used 100 times in the past but it's still apt. Does Allis live here anymore? Back in 1984 I'm sure I saw an Allis around a mile or so beneath Hay on Wye. The Allis is the super shad. The Allis is what every shad fisherman dreams of one day hooking into.

I've talked to numerous people who claim to have seen or hooked or landed an Allis shad. But they have no photographs. Their descriptions are vague. Perhaps they're right, perhaps they're honestly mistaken. I guess there aren't many people who would know an Allis if one bit them on the nose. Sykes, though, is different. In Sykes, I have absolute faith.

Sykes lives in the next village to me, and I've known him 40 years. He's a vast man, heavily bearded, and looks the personification of what he does – an inshore fisherman.

He's eternally tanned, and you can smell the salt on his skin. Sykes knows what he's talking about and when Sykes tells me he's had Allis shads in his nets September time off the Norfolk coast I believe him. Trouble is, like everybody else, Sykes doesn't have the body or the photograph to prove it. That's why I've spent a few days afloat with him. Great days. We've seen all manner of fish. It's been so interesting I've conquered my seasickness. Brilliant. But no Allis. Not yet anyway.

SHAD FACTS

• Treble-hooked spinners for shad have to be a thing of the past. It's vital you unhook shad in the water so as not to disturb those precious scales. For a fly, choose something flashy, about an inch in length. Retrieve quite quickly in fast, erratic jerks. You'll probably experience a lot of taps and nudges and knocks when there are shad around before you get a hammering take. After that, it's fireworks. Just like the tarpon, the junior shad will leave the water again and again in a thrilling aerobatic display.

May 2001. The River Wye, Herefordshire, England.

It's eleven thirty in the morning. I've been out since nine and I've hooked so many Twaite shad that I'm absolutely gasping for a rest. Every one I've believed to be bigger than their eventual weight. Every one has fought like a fish more than twice its size. It's a blissful spring morning. I'm loving it. To be honest, I've caught Twaite with such ease that I don't want to be greedy so that's why I'm sitting on the rocks watching the world go past. There's salmon angler on the opposite bank and I would have given way to him anyway. He's a joy to watch. A good caster always is. He's wielding a 15 foot rod, probably a 10 weight. He's Spey casting his way down the pool, a Labrador at his side. What an art form. He's displaying effortless control, perfect timing, an easy, seamless rhythm. There's never a chance of a salmon in this low water and I'm sure he knows it. He's just glorying in a physical skill expertly executed.

But what's this? He's into something big and surface dancing. The fish comes out once, really high and his shrimp pattern comes adrift. I can see real pain in the man's face. He's calling across to me that it was a grilse, he guesses about seven pounds. He's gutted. But I'm saying it wasn't a grilse. First off, probably, it's too early in the year. But this is the real point. The tail was too forked. There was that blue over silver sheen that I recognized from 20 years back. I'm telling him that fish was an Allis shad, no doubt at all. He shrugs. Probably thinks I'm mad. Allis means nothing to him anyway and he moves on. Now, I fish like a Dervish. For, predictably, absolutely nothing but Twaites. But again I'm a believer.

BLACK BASS *Micropterus salmoides*

Handsome Fighters

Region: North America and Europe

"I am a bass fisherman.

"I have fished for muskie in Lake St. Clair and for tarpon in the Gulf of Mexico. I have fished for pan fish in little ponds and for amber jack off the Islamorada Hump. I have fished for barracuda in the Florida Keys and for King salmon in Alaska. I have fished in 36 states and four foreign countries for virtually every freshwater and saltwater fish known to man. And I can tell you there is no fish anywhere in the world to equal the bass."

From Bass Master, *Shaw Grigsby, 1998.*

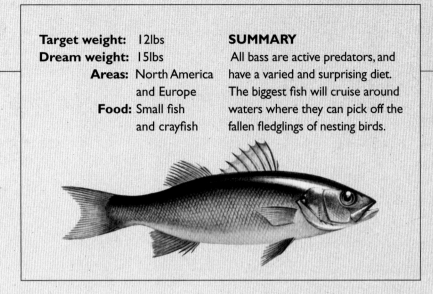

Target weight:	12lbs	**SUMMARY**
Dream weight:	15lbs	All bass are active predators, and
Areas:	North America	have a varied and surprising diet.
	and Europe	The biggest fish will cruise around
Food:	Small fish	waters where they can pick off the
	and crayfish	fallen fledglings of nesting birds.

Shaw is one of hundreds of thousands of American anglers who can't all be wrong. And they're not. Bass are brilliant. They bomb into the 50 because of the fact they were simply built to be fished for. Where they're found, they're plentiful. They're bullish and they're wary in equal measure. That means that sometimes they can pose you so many headaches you want to pack the whole game in. And just when you're about to do this, a big black bass comes out of nowhere and you're in fishing heaven again. You can catch them on the fly, on lure or on bait which, again, is brilliant. It doesn't matter what your favorite method of fishing is or what your mood on any particular day is, the bass will accommodate you. Bass are boldly handsome. Bass fight like bulldogs. That's the large-mouthed bass in a nutshell. Unmissable.

I suppose you've got to say that bass are as American as Cadillacs and I've fished for them in several states, gawping at the gear used and the techniques that have been pioneered. American bass fishermen truly and utterly are leagues apart. But it's this side of the pond that I've had the most fun. You can say what you like about Spain's General Franco – and any student of the Spanish Civil War would have a lot to say about him indeed – but at the very least, he did instigate the huge network of embalsas (reservoirs) throughout the country. And he was a fisherman. He relished salmon, for example, but he also encouraged the introduction of the bass. And it's this Franco innovation that makes you wonder if he were all, completely bad.

by a monstrous bass. The two were circling 10 yards away from me, slowly and ponderously. The large fish as at least six – no seven – times the size of my original. There was no way it could be less than seven or eight pounds. The spectacle went on for four or five minutes and JJ, who was with me, managed to take a photograph. Awesome. Then, suddenly, it was all over. We were shaken and sweaty and beside ourselves.

It wasn't until later when we had the photographs developed – no digital in those days – that we realized that in actual fact the big bass was not trying to consume the smaller one but rather rest the fly away from its jaws. They were, in fact, squabbling over an item of prey. I've seen the same sort of thing on the borders of China where two massive taimen have both attacked a large floating plug. Once, for a minute, I had both fish hooked, each on a separate treble. The combined ferocity of those two fish, though, soon consigned that particular lure to the dustbin.

I've been fortunate to catch bass on spinners, deep plugs, rubber baits, natural baits and flies of all sorts. It's catching bass on the surface, though, that really turns me on.

I have two favorite Spanish black bass waters. One of them is high up in Andalucía, situated in a vast reserve in a fold of the Sierra Morena. You're best having four or five days there, getting to grips with one of the canniest fish species on the planet.

We've got a boat and we potter round the shoreline, exploring the bays. We'll often moor up and move quietly around the rocky areas on foot. You'll find bass very close in, hugging features to them like lovers. If you're quiet you can sometimes look out into the deep, clear water and see the head of a big bass emerging between the rocks.

The lake has good bass in it. For years, we'd been happy with fish between one and three pounds. We once saw a fish that might have been five pounds and I lost one that I swear was four but that was about it as far as we guessed, until this scorching day in late August.

I was in one of the far bays, a place we rarely got to. I was fly fishing with a big yellow lure, so crazy and fluffy I don't think it was ever given a proper name. I was retrieving in a hot, sticky sort of way when it was taken by a decent bass. I could see it struggling in the clear water, perhaps a pound or a pound and a quarter. It was all very pleasant and watching the eagles circling above, I was thinking what a lucky chap I was. Suddenly everything went dull and heavy. I thought for a second I was snagged but the line continued to move. I got up higher on a rock so I could look more penetratingly under the water's surface. My hooked bass had been seized

BLACK BASS FACTS

• The black bass is split into the two species large-mouth and small-mouth. The large-mouth is the larger but many aficionados consider the small-mouth the more sporting and cunning. Small-mouth are found from North Dakota to Quebec, through Oklahoma and into Alabama. They've also been introduced more widely still over the years. You will find large-mouth from Quebec and south to the Gulf. European populations are well scattered with Spanish waters having the largest number of black bass.

March 2004. Andalucia

The four of us have just flown into Malaga airport and Tim is tipsy to the point of being paralytic. Bless him, he simply hates flying and we have to douse him with champagne to get him past the barrier. But now everything's great. Juan is there with the Land Rover and we're on our way into the mountains to the lake, all of us itching to get fishing. And what a view. We hit the heights and then begin our descent down the track towards the cottage, the bay and the boats that are awaiting us. Down at the cottage there's a party going on. It is Sunday afternoon. There's the sound of guitar music. Girls are dancing. We're met by two beautiful women who welcome us. Do we want to drink, or eat or go fishing? There's wine and beer. There's a barbecue sizzling. But the guides are waiting, too, and they say there are bass showing everywhere. The choice is ours. I look at Tim and he's utterly bemused. It's like EasyJet 109 has gone down and he's found himself in paradise. My guide takes me to the top end of the lake, it's a long way and I've never been here before. It's what he calls Bass City because, for half a mile, the area is strewn with dead bushes and trees brought down by the feeder stream in times of winter flood. The electric engine makes barely a sound. You can hear the tinkle of water coming down off the cliffs. You can hear the occasional plop of a bass as it rises to an insect. And you can hear the heat, too, bouncing off the rocks, burning up the vegetation. We agree that I'll fish with a popper. As I say, the best of bassing is on the top. I have my favourite popper. I take him with me everywhere. He's an inch and a half long and green and yellow and he was built to pop. If he wants to he can churn the water to a foam.

There's a skill to working a popper and it always takes me a time to get into the rhythm. You've got to cast out accurately. You've got to leave your popper for 30 seconds. Then, with your rod tip right at the water's surface and with all the slack line gathered tight, you give the popper a six inch tug. It should be dynamic. It should make a statement. Then you leave your popper again. Another 30 seconds, perhaps more and repeat the process. A bass might come at any moment. It's heart stopping. Your mouth's dry. Sweat's sluicing off you.

Now we're on our fourth bush. The third was a disaster. I'd cast my popper fast into the branches and we'd had to motor right in to retrieve it. No way am I ever going to lose him. But now I feel in the zone. I've got my casting action back. My popping is back to its best. Mr. Popper is riding the surface exactly where I want him. Down goes my rod tip. I ever so gently gather in the slack. And then I pop him. And he responds dramatically. I let him settle and then he's gone in a fast eruption of water. This is what I love about bass. I love being above them in a boat, seeing the rod bend crazily, feeling it actually bend under the butt. Okay, it's great to see bass thrashing on the surface but it's even better to feel them powering, boring, bulldozing their way towards the roots of a tree and safety. How I hang on to this fish I just can't tell you. I want to go yee-ha and throw my Stetson high in the sky. This is like riding in a rodeo. Suddenly, the heart goes out of him. He swirls a bit on the surface, tries another half-hearted jump and we scoop him out.

He's massive. He's nearly five pounds. My guide holds him, smiling and I click off just a couple of photographs. No more because of the heat of the sun on his flanks. We put him back and he doesn't loiter! He's gone before you can blink. No, I don't want to fish on thank you. We potter back to the party. I dance awhile and drink awhile and the stars come out. The other members of my gang join me. We sit on a bench by the waterside. We've all caught bass. Fishing just doesn't come better.

RAINBOW TROUT

Oncorhynchus mykiss

Big Hearted Fish

Region: Worldwide

"One of the first things I observed as a visitor in the new frontier was that everything was big. Alaska boasts Mount McKinley at over 20,000 feet the highest peak in North America, as well as Kodiak bears, golden eagles and enormous moose. I was as displeased to find that the mosquitoes follow this pattern as I was pleased that the native rainbows did too. Anglers come from around the world to Alaska – famous for its runs of five species of salmon as well as for the Dolly Varden, Arctic char and the largest grayling in the world. But its greatest game fish is arguably the rainbow trout."

From Trout – An Illustrated History *James Prosek, 1996.*

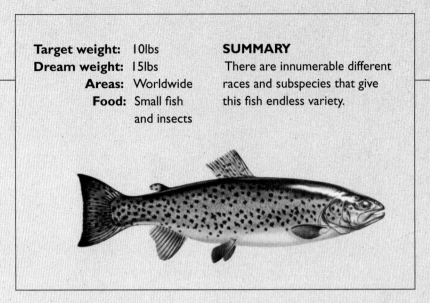

Target weight:	10lbs	**SUMMARY**
Dream weight:	15lbs	There are innumerable different
Areas:	Worldwide	races and subspecies that give
Food:	Small fish	this fish endless variety.
	and insects	

I like that. It says a lot about rainbows up that way. I haven't fished Alaska – the furthest up the west coast I've got is British Columbia and the Yukon but I've met up with some pretty big hearted rainbows there, too. There's a lake north of Prince Rupert, I remember, completely surrounded by forest that Big Bob took me to. So remote that we had to get in there by boat plane. The water was gin. An overworked term, I know, but here the only word to use. You could see your fly 15 yards down. You could see massive rainbows cruising close to the bottom that were a world away. They hit like hammers. They fought forever. Perfect coloring. Perfect fins. Perfect fish. They were all generosity, honesty, everything you'd expect from one of the world's favorite three or four fish. Rainbow trout do exactly what they promise. They're not like browns. They don't sulk, they don't go moody, and when they're hooked they don't hug the bottom. Rainbows are always up for it, always there to give an angler a chance, to give him the time of his life.

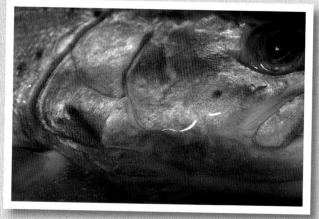

That's how a rainbow trout got me in Slovenia in November 2007. A crackling cold day in the forest, the river running quick and clear through the trees. I'd stalked fish throughout the morning before I found this one, a rainbow, perhaps eight pounds, close to the bank, feeding gustily from the drift. How long I watched that fish I don't know. It glowed. There was a vibrancy about it, an exuberance. Al tried to catch it. The moment his fly landed and skated cross current towards the fish's nose, it was off, a missile downstream. I love Al but I was glad. That fish was better seen in the water.

For the most part, we've been talking wild rainbows, fish that have nothing to do with hatcheries and it's tempting to be snooty, to dub them in some way superior. It's easy to forget that the humble stew pond rainbow stocked into endless commercial fisheries around the world have given so much pleasure to so many anglers… me included.

I can't not be reminded of my great angling companion, Reel Screamer. Then, well over quarter of a century ago, he was new to the fly fishing game and I'd taken him to the most exclusive trout lake in southern England. Our host, titled of course, had appeared with his wife on the far side of the lake so I felt it only courteous to leave Reel Screamer to his unproductive thrashings and go and deliver out thanks. The lake was a large one and the day was hot so it took me 10 minutes to reach their fishing hut. No sooner had I arrived and been offered tea when pandemonium broke out on the far bank. Reel Screamer was into a large rainbow and he was unaided. We could only watch. I could only pray.

Within a minute, Reel Screamer was wrapped up in line, like a large, pink Christmas parcel. Another minute on and he was in the shallows, wading after the floundering fish, a grizzly hunting a spawning salmon. He lunged at the fish, rugby-style, disappearing from view but when he resurfaced, a five pound flapping rainbow was clutched to his heaving bosom. "Yes, yes, yes" he screamed, punching the air. In the hut, the silence was deafening. After a frozen half minute, my host turned to me, "Very enthusiastic, your friend," he said. That's how rainbow trout get you.

That's how they got me on New Zealand's north island back in the 90s. Ken had taken me to a small stream early in the morning and there lay three rainbow trout the like of which I'll never see again. They were huge, yes, but that was beside the point. It was their magnificence that dumbfounded me. Their poise. Their coloring. Their sheer majesty.

RAINBOW TROUT FACTS

• I like the versatility of rainbow trout. Some of the finest ones I've personally met with have been those that have gone to sea. They're not steelheads exactly but landlubbers who've established a good living in estuaries and brackish creeks around. Here, they live on crabs, sand eels, whiting and the like and grow very big and silvery indeed. But that's the rainbow. A survivor. Make the best of life.

June 1979. Edgefield Lake, North Norfolk, England.

It's been a wet, mild, windless sort of day and now, at eight p.m. the rain has died away to become a mere freckling on the surface of the lake. There is no hint of a breeze. The mist of rain comes down vertical. A spider's web wouldn't tremble. The lake here is a mirror apart from where it's broken by the purposeful activity of rainbow trout. Conditions are perfect for my purpose.

I've been reading the trout fishers' book of the decade, perhaps of the century. Brian Clarke's *Pursuit of Stillwater Trout*. Clarke has inspired us all. I've been following in his footsteps and now, tonight, I'm here to step another rung up the ladder. I'm going to catch a rainbow trout on a buzzer. Or at least I'm praying I do so. I've exhausted my patience stripping back Baby Dolls and massive creations of fluff and fantasy. Now, as Clarke is urging me to do, I'm after the real rainbow experience.

I'm doing what he says. I'm watching the water in front of me intently. I'm studying the patrol routes of individual fish. I'm sinking into their world. Nothing else exists for me. I'm still a teacher. I've got problems with two kids wanting to go to Cambridge but that's all forgotten. It's me and the rainbow trout and my five-weight outfit, a size 16, red buzzer on the point.

It's a specific fish now, at eight thirty, I'm homing in on. It looks a beauty. Two and a half pounds. I've got its patrol route nailed. I know exactly where to place my fly. There's Edgefield Hall reflected on the surface and I know that when my rainbow swims through the sitting room, I've got to place my buzzer a yard away, to the right, exactly on the roof of the coal sheds.

The cast is okay. I have 45 seconds to wait. The rainbow's approaching in the surface layers. I can see its dorsal.

Sometimes its shoulders. A foot. Nine inches. Eight. Seven. I twitch the fly line. The buzzer rises. The rainbow sees, flicks to its left. The leader jabs forward. I lift into my fish. The hall explodes into ruins as the fish leaps, galvanized, deceived. My breakthrough, my immense achievement.

BROWN TROUT *Salmo trutta*

Effortless Nobility
Region: North and South America, Europe, Asia, and Australasia

"Refrigeration. Steam. Victorian ingenuity in every field. From the later 19th century, brown trout got everywhere. North America. South America. India. Kashmir. New Zealand. Australia. Africa. I guess now, there are seven countries in the world where you can't catch a brown trout though I'm happy to be proved wrong. Perhaps they are the world's favorite fish."

From How Trout Conquered the World *John Bailey book proposal 2002.*

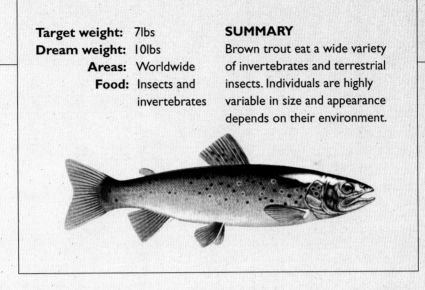

Target weight: 7lbs
Dream weight: 10lbs
Areas: Worldwide
Food: Insects and invertebrates

SUMMARY
Brown trout eat a wide variety of invertebrates and terrestrial insects. Individuals are highly variable in size and appearance depends on their environment.

The world's favorite fish? Probably. Even if an angler isn't targeting a brown, if he catches one, then he's invariably pleased. The phrase "had a good brownie" is pretty well universal. Everyone talks of a brown trout with this type of affection. Brown trout are, in some particular fishy way of theirs, noble without being snobby or aristocratic. They're accessible but they're aesthetically unbeatable. And the lovely thing about brown trout is that an angler can never say he knows them absolutely. There are just so many different strains, so many different colors and spotting patterns, so many variations on the original wonderous theme.

Take Lough Corrib in southwest Ireland. I well remember one of the guides telling me there were at least two dozen quite distinct strains of trout within the lough. You could show this man a brown trout, and he could tell you exactly from which part of the lough the fish had been caught. You can never tire of brown trout. There's always a surprise left in them. I have caught brown trout from scores if not hundreds of different venues: I've never been disappointed, and frequently I've been stunned.

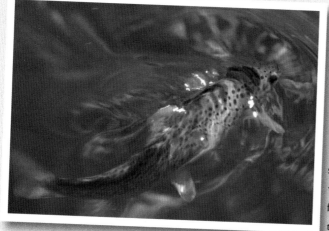

have to resort to fly fishing tactics that bear no resemblance whatsoever to the norm. You've got to move so slowly and carefully that you might just as well be a tortoise. You've got to use every shard of cover available. You've got to consider the angle of the sun. Most of the time you will have the very maximum of a meter or so of fly line out from the rod tip. Fly line on the water spells disaster. If you are using a dry fly, the leader will have to be sunk – no point at all having any floating on the surface. And if at all possible, fish that dry fly OFF the water's surface itself. Yes, if you can manage it, under trees especially, have your dry hanging vertically from you rod tip and let it skip on the surface, barely freckling it, always in control, waiting for a fish to hook itself, often three or six inches clear of the surface. Fish conventionally and you are doomed. And all this for a brownie rarely eight inches long.

And they're cunning. To catch a brown trout, an educated one, you've got to fish well. Many years ago, on my local river, before I developed scruples, there were always pods of nice, wild brownies. They rarely exceeded two and a half pounds in weight but that didn't matter. They were beautiful and they were challenging. In those days, I'd kick off fly fishing. Just perhaps I'd extract a fish or two but the going would be invariably tough. I'd then resort to bait. Yes, I admit it. Not that mostly it did me much good at all.

You'd think a small dead fish trundled through their lies would instantly be accepted. Sometimes yes, sometimes no. There would never be any guarantees. Even if I went gossamer light – say a two pound tippet and an 18 hook and fished maggots, they still weren't easy, never a pushover. I might extract a fish but then they'd close down on me. They'd learn to move out of the way if a hooked maggot drifted in front of their noses, no matter how cunningly presented.

I've known wild browns down in the crystal clear streams of southwest England prove just as difficult. Sometimes they're so invisible it's only their shadow cast on the river bed by the sun that gives them away. The sound and sight of a fly line landing anywhere near them in bright conditions is enough to kill a stretch of water for hours. Leaders laughed at. Artificials are examined if you're lucky, generally they're ignored. Laughed at. On waters like these, the only times I've caught anything at all is after heavy rain when the waters have clouded.

If you're to catch one under normal conditions then you

BROWN TROUT FACTS

• We have made a great deal about the different strains of wild brown trout. This is not surprising. Tests done around Pitlochry in Scotland have shown that wild brown trout in a loch always return to their natal feeder stream. They hatch out, grow, move into the loch, mature and then return to the same stream where they were born. Ferox trout are typical of this behavior. Ferox only spawn with ferox and perhaps this is how they maintain their genetic purity.

September 1989. The Kingie River, Invernesshire, Scotland.

I've just come back from some weeks of glorious brown trout fishing in Kashmir. I'm bronzed and healthy. I'm deflated to be back in the UK. I need a challenge and Gordon gives me one. We move from the bar into the map room. This is how he sees it. "Get out early tomorrow. Drive up to Loch Quoich. Take the boat on the north side of the loch and motor to the big bay on the south, just up from the dam. Then it's a long walk over into the Kingie valley. I guess you'll be looking at two, probably three miles but taking that boat trip of yours saves you at least four or five miles of a walk in. That's why I guess nobody has ever been before. Certainly not within my memory. Perhaps not within anyone's memory. There's a challenge for you, you moping, bloody Englishman!"

The alarm clock has just rung. It's barely light. I'm out of the sleeping hotel and up the single track road to where I know the boat is lying. There's a brisk wind from the west and crossing the loch isn't as easy as I would like it. There's also rain coming in on the wind. It's cold for the time of year.

I beach. I walk briskly over a steep ridge, down into a shallow valley, up another ridge and then, at last, towards the Kingie River itself. So close to its source, the river is small but violent, untamed. I'm loving it already.

The rut isn't quite on us but it's close. There are stags beginning to roar. The moor is settling into its autumn coat. And, as Gordon said I would be, I'm quite, quite alone.

Apart from fish. For six hours, I fish every pool and every riffle and every cast, virtually yields a fish. These are trout between eight ounces and perhaps, just, three pounds. They are fin perfect. Untouched by man. Their colors are every shade of yellow, red, scarlet and brown. When I return them, they melt back to the depths of their pool. Bemused, angry with themselves. They'll never be fooled again.

It's already four in the afternoon. I take two fish which I know Gordon will cook for my supper and retrace my steps back towards the shore of Quoich. The boat's engine fires and I'm relieved because, by now, the day is giving way to night and I don't want to tackle the wide crossing in the dark. The gloom is thick by the time I beach. I'm driving my way down the narrow, serpentine road towards the distant lights of the hotel. And my heart is full and happy. Seventy fish perhaps. All on tiny nymphs or miniscule dries.

Gordon sees my face when I walk into the bar and he smiles broadly. The sort of day I've had shines out of me. We'll have Champagne with our fish.

STEELHEAD Salmo gairdneri

Kind of Mystical

Region: North American west coast

"On the seventh day, I watched Bob, the big bearded guide and hunter hold the head of my fresh-run female steelhead against the current until she was recovered. I felt the water splashed by her tail against my face, saw her streak like a star back into the crystal waters of the Kwinimass, and knew I was casting in the fisherman's heaven. Seeing the look in my eyes, big, grizzled Bob says, 'Kinda mystical ain't they?'"

From John Bailey's fishing diary, Canada, 1996.

Target weight:	20lbs	**SUMMARY**
Dream weight:	25lbs	Steelhead grow very large on a
Areas:	North America	marine diet – have a strong silver
Food:	Small fish	sheen when they return to their
		natal river. This fades after time
		in freshwater.

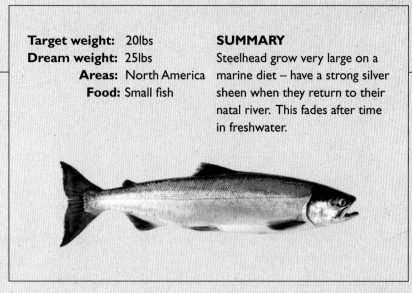

Steelhead make the 50 list for their obvious magnificent qualities – they are one of the most fabulously beautiful, massively spirited trout species on the planet. But they're also there for what they represent. In the past, I've described them as icon fish – fish that evoke so much in us as anglers. They're beacons of hope for a better environmental future. They're living reminders of our wavering natural heritage. Every steelhead river in crisis is a call to our conscience. Steelhead are predominantly fish of the west coast of North America and Canada, and too many of their rivers have been laid waste by logging, mining, and hydro-electric development. Their most eloquent spokesman is Mark Hume. His book *Run of the River* is a must read. Beg it. Borrow it. Steal it. Remember it.

Above all, read it. "Rivers spin our turbines, powering industry and lighting the cities. They carry away our industrial and residential waste. But they do not wash away our sins. Long before the environmental stress on a river becomes obvious to most of us, it shows up in the fish. They're canaries in a mine – but canaries that cannot sing. We must pay attention to what the fish are telling us and to the whisper in voices of our rivers, for they are speaking about our future...the history of the ocean and the earth is written on the skin of steelhead, etched in the scales. I pushed her back into the river so she could tell her story to the glaciers." How can you ignore writing like this?

We lived in his old fishing boat in the estuary of the river and, each night, ate crabs and lobsters caught from the water beneath us, talked a great deal and, generally, got very drunk. Above deck, a canopy of stars spangled over our boat. The air was so still you could hear the bears, recently emerged from their hibernation, fighting and snarling over territory. It was a good life. So, too, was the fishing.

Dawn on the fourth day was particularly magnificent. The mountains had received a fresh dusting of snow through the night but now the sky was spectacularly blue. It was early and we pushed up the river in Bob's big power boat in air that was still freezing. We ground our way through the rapids, and we surged through the pools, the Kwinimass becoming smaller and smaller before us. There, at last, in the woods, lay one of Bob's great pools, one of the world's great steelhead locations.

We beached the boat low down the stream from the pool, and I crept along the shoreline, put out a cast, and hooked a fish at once that ran and ran, jumped, and broke me within 15 seconds. I sat in agony until I remembered what Bob had said, how steelhead are the nomads of the sea, keeping always a fin-beat ahead of their many enemies. These are not ordinary fish: it's no disgrace to lose out to a steelhead.

The steelhead is in essence a rainbow trout, but one that makes its way to the sea. After hatching, steelhead spend their first two or even three years living in the rivers of their birth but then turn into smolts and prepare for their life in the salt. They will feed there for anything between one and three years before returning to spawn. Unlike Pacific salmon many, perhaps the majority of steelhead, survive, return to the sea and come back to spawn on more occasions.

Most migrating steelhead head for the north Pacific, past the Aleutian Islands, following the ocean currents. According to Bob, they swim deep in the seas, searching the cold, feeding on prawn and shrimp. Seals are their enemies and killer whales, too. And, along the way, they also run the gauntlet of the gill net boats, fishing for the species of Pacific salmon that accompany them. The ocean's dangers are immense.

This affinity to the sea in many ways defines the steelhead. It is the element of the ocean that explains its size, its power, its vivacity. The sea reflects in every shining scale, it vibrates in every fiber of the fish's being. It's like the surge of the tides is driving that first unstoppable run that is one of the many glories of this species for the fisherman.

It was largely Mark Hume's book that drew me to the Kwinimass in the first place back in the mid nineties. Bob, I had been told, was the man to go with. And he was.

STEELHEAD FACTS

• The true steelhead is an aristocratic fish that has quite defined divisions in its life between the fresh and the salt. Its classic life pattern dictates important and dramatic migrations. However, many stocked rainbow trout do find their way down their water courses to the sea where they will live a productive life in the estuary. They mooch in and out with the tides growing big on a marine diet. While not true steelheads, they become silvery in color and can easily double or treble their weight.

May 1996. The Kwinimass River.

I've been seeing many steelhead in my first five and six days on the river. They're like ghosts, phantoms, mirages I can't quite grasp. On the second night, I round a bend and there, howling at the moon, sits a pack of wolves. A steelhead jumps, big and black in the silver light and the splashing stops their singing. Each day I see numbers of fish, traveling just as Bob says, in pairs. Males and females together, pushing up stream towards the spawning redds. Always, these steelhead have been desperately difficult to approach, spooky in the crystal water, aware of the boat, darting away at the crunch of a wader and sinking deep down into a pool at the whistle of fly line overhead. Now, I'm despairing of ever catching one. Bob tells me to have confidence, to believe. He says I've got to fish the tails of the pools with absolute care and concentration. It's here, in that steady push of water, just where the deeps and shallows meet and the current is exactly to their liking that the fish will lie. This is why he's put me now at the tail of the run beneath the snow-capped mountain.

I can't believe it when the hook finally connects. The fish runs everywhere at once. I'm totally out of control. I've never been in contact with a fish like this. Even now, close to the end, after 20 bruising minutes, her last runs come with such power that I feel like weeping. I look at Bob, pleadingly. Will this fish never give up? Now she does and I realize that I'm looking at the most handsome fish I've ever seen. Or guessed I would see. I don't want to fish on. To do so, would be an abuse of her glory but Bob puts the rod back in my hands and next cast, I take her mate. Perhaps he was lovelorn. He, too, goes back at once and the two are reunited. The loveliest thing of all is that only two minutes later, two big steelhead, a male and a female, leave the pool and crash their way through the shallows ever onwards towards their destiny.

ARCTIC CHAR *Salvelinus alpinus*

The Most Beautiful of Fish

Region: Alaska, Northern Canada, Russia, Britain, Ireland, Scandinavia, Greenland, and Iceland

A fish can be free-biting. A fish can be hard fighting. But with the char, you simply want to catch it because of its beauty. There has to be the world's most beautiful fish just as there is the world's most beautiful woman. And the char is that fish.

From John Bailey's fishing diary, Greenland, 1996.

Target weight: 6lbs
Dream weight: 10lbs
Areas: Upper north hemisphere
Food: Small fish, shrimp, and sand eels.

SUMMARY

In the sea, char eat all manner of shrimp, sand eel, and small fish. This rich diet gives the fish vitality and huge growth potential.

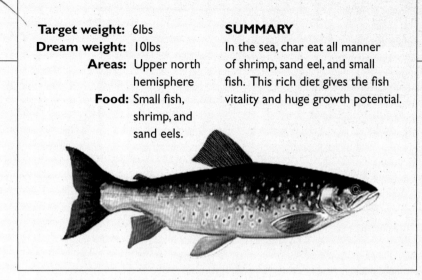

As ever, there are caveats. Landlocked char, left in deep, glacial lakes all over northern Europe after the retreat of the Ice Cap, are comparatively small, pallid, insipid little things. They might have a charm but they're very rarely the sort of creatures that make your jaw drop. Seagoing char, however, are from a different planet.

You can catch seagoing char down the east coast of Canada. You can catch them around Iceland. But, best of all, worldwide, the most beautiful Arctic Char are to be found on the west coast rivers of Greenland.

Char here seem to reflect the essentials of Greenland itself. There's a purity to their coloring and a streamlined lack of clutter to their shape, which are both eye-bogglingly gorgeous. But how do you describe the colors of these fish? It's pretty well beyond me. I don't think there are enough words in any vocabulary to describe the different shades that the char exhibit. And, of course, male and female both show different colorings. The males, in particular, can at times have bellies that look as though they're on fire! Orange isn't the word, neither is crimson or scarlet. This color is a vibrant, throbbing flame! And the females can be anything from pink to yellow to vermillion to any one of 1,000 shades of green or blue or lemon.

And what makes these west Greenlandic char so phenomenal? Perhaps it's the rich feed in the seas that they inhabit. They're feasting on shrimps and prawns and krill and sand-eels and elvers and 1,000 other oceanic creatures that nourish them with brimming life. And then they leave the sea to run the short rivers towards the Ice Cap where they spawn sometime in the late summer. Often these rivers are often five or ten miles long, crystal pure, sometimes with the very ice from the Ice Cap floating in the current. Can there be wilder, purer, more ancient waters than these?

So this is why you've got to pursue Arctic Char in Greenland. This is the prime reason that they have bombed their way into the 50 list. As I hinted, they do take flies with gusto — not that they're stupid and not that the crystal clear water doesn't give them the edge. At times, they will come up for the dry fly but, generally, they love to hammer into small, red lures that presumably remind them of shrimps.

Once hooked, then, by God, do they fight! A four pounder can make a blur of your reel. An eight pounder is more rocket than fish. Ten pounds, as far as I've found, seems to be about as big as these fish get, but if they were bigger, you'd simply never land them. They'd break your bones before they'd let you.

Fishing in Greenland demands extreme resilience from the angler. This is the loneliest, largest island in the world. I've spent three weeks there and not seen a single passing stranger. No roads. No tracks. Nothing but seashore, river, tundra, and Ice Cap. You might see a deer or a musk ox or an Arctic fox but human beings, forget it. For this reason alone, you're thrown totally onto your own resources in Greenland. Lose your gear, you can forget a tackle shop. Run out of food, there's hardly likely to be a supermarket. At least you can drink from the rivers in the summer, the milky-white nights of the midnight sun means there is no need for your torch.

ARCTIC CHAR FACTS

• You can tell char from salmon by their coloration. Char have light markings on the darker background whereas salmon and trout have dark markings on a lighter background. Char are very much creatures of cool water, belonging to glacial lakes, cold seas, and cold rivers.

• Arctic char are found above latitude 64° north. They winter in the sea and move into fresh water to spawn throughout the summer.

July, 1996. Paradise Valley, Greenland.

Johnny and I have been in Paradise Valley fishing the river of the same name for two weeks now. It's like we know all the pools and runs and the river is an old friend to us. But we're wrong. Paradise has a last, wonderful secret. Today, I walked way up stream, past our normal stopping point. The river peters to nothing. It's simply a few inches deep running around boulders. It was just that a little voice kept urging me on. I'd covered a mile, I was now a good five miles from camp and I noticed the water beginning to deepen somewhat. And then, unexpectedly, quite in the middle of nowhere, in the shadow of the glacier itself, the run deepened and strengthened and there were the fish. These are the biggest char of them all. The run is 100 yards long, narrow, deep, crystal and the char are lined up, in rows, males, red-coated like 18th century soldiers. These are huge, angry fish. I cast out a spinner and four big fish wheeled round to chase it, harry it from the area. The largest took. The fight was volcanic. Then, finally, it lay at my feet and I realized I was looking at the most wondrous fish it's ever been my privilege to see. Never can there have been a char as handsome as this. Ten pounds, I guess. Bristling defiance. Orange flanks that simply pulsated.

I immediately walked the five miles back to camp, found Johnny, and walked the five miles again to show him the pool. He caught a fish to match mine and now we're back in our camp, exhausted, exultant, and confident we have found the most special place on the most special river in Greenland.

There are shadows now all round the valley. I close my eyes. What I know is that never again will I have a better day's fishing than this. These are days spent in heaven, not on earth.

HUCHEN

Hucho hucho

Cornerstone of the 50

Region: Eastern and Central European river systems

"Many of the pictures in the old man's room were unconnected with the complex and bitter history of middle Europe. They showed anglers in the sporting garb of the 1920s and 1930 on the banks of turbulent, Slovak rivers: the Vah, the Orava, the Turiek. Held up for the camera, often by two anglers because one could not manage it alone, were great, beautiful fish. Some of them looked to be 50 or 60 pounds and the adipose fins that they displayed showed clearly that they were members of the salmon family. They were more rakishly built, though, than any trout species or sea going salmon, with a meaner look about the head and the jaws. The photographs were black and white or dull sepia that failed to show the copper-green luster of the flanks fading to pink, the peppering of tiny dark spots, the silver bellies of the living fish."

I Know a Good Place, *Clive Gammon, 1989.*

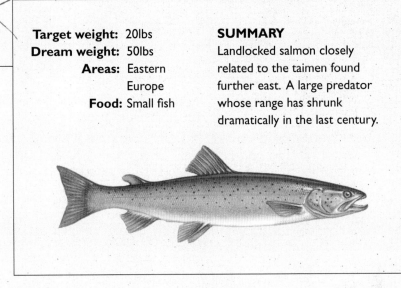

Target weight: 20lbs
Dream weight: 50lbs
Areas: Eastern Europe
Food: Small fish

SUMMARY
Landlocked salmon closely related to the taimen found further east. A large predator whose range has shrunk dramatically in the last century.

Hucho hucho. Huchen. Danubian salmon. It's your choice of name and it could well be a fish you've never heard of, so you're wondering why it's such a cornerstone of the 50. There are several reasons. For one, as the introductory piece makes clear, huchen have been so long out of reach to virtually anyone in the west or in America. For most of the 20th century, the best huchen rivers ran through areas impossible to reach. The previously Communist-run countries like Slovakia and Hungary where tourists, even anglers, were hardly welcomed were out of bounds.

Of course, there were always hallowed huchen waters in Austria and south Germany, but these were preserved, barely talked about, and almost exclusively for rich locals.

Furthermore, for much of the 20th century, too, huchen seemed to be a declining species. I suspect that from the '60s to the '80s, every passing year slimmed down my chances. I heard rumours that under the Communists, huchen hatcheries were being starved of cash and failing. Also, the increase in hydro-electric schemes impeded the routes of spawning huchen.

So, for so much of my life, there's been the sheer mystery of where I would ever find a huchen to actually fish for. One of its names, the Danubian salmon, suggests that the Danube catchment area is at the heart of the action. True to a degree but the Danube itself has long been too dirty, too messed about with to be home to them. Its tributaries, though, in Austria, Slovenia, Hungary, and perhaps Croatia and Bosnia are the places to go looking now the 21st century politics have given us new horizons.

The biology of the huchen is important in its inclusion, of course. There's a record of a fish weighing over 230 pounds in 1943. Almost unbelievably large. At that weight, we are conceivably talking about the largest salmon in the world and that's a huge attraction in its own right. The huchen's vomerine teeth suggest it's more akin to the char family than to the salmons but I think this is being too picky. As far as I'm concerned, the huchen is a massive, handsome, mysterious, land-locked salmon.

Family history plays a part. I had a grandfather who was a passionate fisherman and, to my regret died almost 20 years before I was born. However, my grandmother who accompanied him to the riverbank for many decades of their relationship, lived on to be the first person to put a rod into my hand. From her I picked up many of the family's angling legends not least of which were the stories of my grandfather's expeditions after the huchen in the River Thames, England. In the first decade of the 20th century, there were considerable movements of fish species around the world, and one of the most entertaining was the transportation of the huchen from the Danubian area to the River Thames. It appears that a sizable number of small huchen were released in several of the Thames weir pools and they swam away never to be seen again. For many years, it appeared that this was one experiment that could be consigned to the dustbin.

Then, around the very late 1920s, stories began to percolate of pike anglers fishing in the winter and being smashed repeatedly by enormous, unseen giants. The timing would fit. These fish, then, would be about

20 years old and the huchen is comparatively slow growing. It takes them that amount of time to reach 40 or 50 pounds in weight and at that size they would obviously be more than a match for any angler out to catch the odd jack for the pot. By the winter of 1932/1933, my grandfather, who was a very keen pike angler, found the stories impossible to resist. He was then a mill owner in Bradford and through the course of that period made several journeys with my grandmother south in their gleaming new Daimler car. They would put up at a hotel and my grandfather would spend day after day spinning his lures or swimming his live bait round the weir pools. Each time they went home fishless. He caught pike, big perch, and one or two large Thames cannibal trout, but the huchen evaded him. The story goes, though, that he saw one. Some cold evening, he was bringing in a large silver spoon when a shape three times the size of any pike was seen following it. The fish closed, turned, and bulleted back into the deep, dark water. The sighting was quite enough to make grandfather determined he would be back. Sadly, he wasn't. He tripped, fell, and died some months afterwards.

HUCHEN FACTS

• The huchen is a particularly active hunter after darkness, with the majority of its food made up of loach and bullheads, which come out at night to prey on invertebrates, and that's when these small fish are vulnerable to the big, hunting huchen. If fishing is allowed, that first hour of darkness is probably the best chance for the biggest fish. Don't neglect a three inch long squat, mottled bullhead pattern, either fly or lure, fished slowly bouncing the bottom.

December 2007, Slovenia.

Gaze on this photograph of Al and his fish because this is what it's all about. True, Al's fish isn't a 50 or a 60 pounder. It weighs 22 pounds but that's still enough to put it into the league of the desirable. As far as I'm concerned, it's close to being the unattainable. December 1st, a Saturday, was quite a day. We began on our river at dawn. The water smoked. There was heavy frost all around. The cottages and the gardens alongside the river looked all Hansel and Gretel and quaint. The forests were silent. Our small group barely spoke. It was as though we all knew we were on the edge of something miraculous.

As the light grew, Al hollered out. We could hear his reel. We could hear a big fish splashing far, far out in the pool. We all ran to him with nets, cameras, good advice. We found him slumped against a tree trunk, the rod on the ground, the line limp. It had been on for a minute, he said, and taken perhaps 20 or 30 yards of line. It had felt like a crocodile. This was my fifth trip to Slovenia and I'd never been so close to seeing the huchen. I was at least as wretched as Al.

Lunch was a quiet affair. Rok, our guide, was optimistic about the coming evening but I felt lightning was unlikely to strike twice. We were to split up. Some of us went back to the Great Pool and others to the Old Road Bridge, the place we'd seen fish earlier in the week. That was where Al chose to fish. With his second cast, as the light was fading, he hooked another fish. It broke him almost immediately. His devastation was total. He walked in the woods for half an hour, kicking the dead leaves, mulling over his misery. He knew deep down that he hadn't done anything really wrong, just that luck hadn't been on his side. Perhaps it was this thought that made him tackle up again.

Almost at once, unbelievably, Al was into his third fish of the day. And this one, despite its power, its aerobatics, the frenzy of its fight, did not come off. This fish stuck and as I took photographs of it in the intense blackness of the forest, I was as dazed as Al, overjoyed that my family's search had come to its conclusion.

TAIMEN
Hucho taimen

The Greatest Salmonoid

Region: Asia

"The taimen is the oldest form of salmonid in existence. It's also the largest, the rarest, and the least scientifically researched. This is a magnificent creature swimming on the very limits of our imagination, inspiring us to the ultimate of angling challenges."

From John Bailey's fishing diary, Siberia, 1994.

Target weight:	20lbs	**SUMMARY**
Dream weight:	100lbs	A fish of fast rivers and deep
Areas:	Mongolia and	cold lakes. Spends much of the
	Siberia, Russia	year under ice. Feeds voraciously
Food:	Fish, rodents,	on lenok trout and white fish.
	and birds	

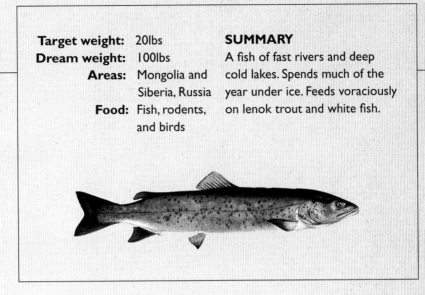

The taimen can be found throughout Siberia, even as far as the Sea of Japan, but it is in Mongolia that it has its present day stronghold. The isolated, near-uninhabited wastes of this country suit the taimen well. In Siberia, the taimen has been hunted near to extinction because of its size – perhaps up to 150 pounds – and its eating qualities. In Mongolia, this ancient, slow-growing, almost mythical fish finds safety.

Taimen are huge predators. They can be taken equally on fly or artificial lure. They fight magnificently. With their splendid orange or crimson tails they are beautiful to look at in a menacing, brooding fashion. Days can be electric, it's as though every fish in the river is on the prowl. And if you're not catching taimen, there are the magnificent Mongolian grayling to hunt for or the large, game, splendidly spotted lenok trout. Mongolia, truly, is an angler's paradise.

The best of the taimen fishing is before the snows, before the bone-cracking cold of the winter sets in. Nights plummet to -4F (-20°C). Frosts lie half an inch thick. The larch forests turn from green to brown to gold. As the sun rises and the skies turn to aching blue, the snow-capped mountain peaks dazzle like beacons. The air is pure, still, and rings with silence. This is why you go taimen fishing.

Perhaps you ride to your fishing on a sturdy, Mongolian pony. You will gallop across endless steppe. You might see wolves, traces of bear, wild boar, deer, everything but man. Perhaps a storm will blow in from Siberia, and the clouds will turn the color of cygnet down. The skies will fill with snow, and for a while you'll shelter in the forest, build yourself a fire, and talk about fishing. Then the sun will shine once more, you'll hook a taimen, and gallop back to the ger (the white, traditional tent of Mongolia) to celebrate long into the star-spangled night.

In the ger, you'll drink, you'll dance, you'll sing, you will arm-wrestle with your host. You will feast of stew of yak meat and drink their vodka. And when you go outside to wash in the river, you'll look up and the sky will be a planetarium, open just for you, admission free.

That's why you go fishing for taimen. That's why you travel seemingly to the ends of the earth, not just for a fish but to rediscover the beginnings of that earth. Whoever you are in the west, you're simply a man in Mongolia like all others, struggling for existence. This is the world as it was when it was proud and untamed.

TAIMEN FACTS

• Taimen are generally measured rather than weighed. A fish of a three feet is considered good. Three and a half feet is a specimen and anything over four feet is considered very large indeed. There are reports of fish over five feet or even up to six and a half feet. Fish like this, though, are rare as the tomb of Genghis Khan.

August 2000. Shiskid River, North West Mongolia.

I'd heard about the Power Station Pool from passing hunters who told me of it year upon year. Down there, they'd always pointed, to where the river disappears into the mountains. On, on, they would say, flapping their arms. Huge fish. Many of them, they'd promise. The place where the river narrows and thunders through its gorge. There I'd catch my monster.

The day came. I'd had enough of dreams. I set out alone perhaps half an hour before dawn. The night was black but for 10 miles I knew my way. By 9am though, I was in new territory, moving fast through the thickening forest. Keeping the river to my right, I moved on with difficulty, throughout the morning. All paths had disappeared. The forest was dense, dark, looming and stank of bear. By mid-day, I'd been walking six hours and was preparing to turn round, defeated, when I heard it.

In the distance, I could hear a roar, a primeval sound, as though the earth itself was bellowing. The Power Station Pool! Within half an hour, I was there, above it, looking down on the foaming, rushing water. Taimen were there beneath me in rows, 40 fish perhaps. Or 50. Their orange tails beat the current as though they were marching in time to a drummer. And they were big fish. Some were monsters.

I got down to the water's edge. I put on an orange Shadrap, perhaps seven inches long and cast it far, far out into the Pool. The current was swift and spray from the falls floated in the air. One bow wave, two bow waves followed my lure in but turned away and shot back into the Pool. The second cast nothing, the third cast a blank. The fourth cast and my rod pulled over like it had been hit by a sandbag. The fish fought me for an hour and 10. It took me half a mile down the river. At one stage it had over 200 meters of line from my reel. I never felt remotely in control of that fish, not until I had it in the shallows, a stringer tethering it to a boulder the size of a small car.

I looked at my watch. It was nearly three o'clock. I had five hours of walking ahead of me and darkness would fall at seven. This fishing trip had become desperate. As the moon rose, I was still five miles from the camp and the silhouettes of six wolves appeared on the ridge to my right. They trailed me as far as the stream two miles from the camp but there I was met by Batsokh, waving his lantern, firing off his gun. I fell into his arms and, back at the camp, told them all my story.

The next day, Batsokh and Gamba accompanied me back to the Power Station. We took photographs of the great fish and released it. They begged me to cast again but to do so would have broken the spell of the place. I've never been back. You can't keep living miracles.

GOLDEN DORADO *Salminus maxillosus*

The Fighter in Gold

Region: South American freshwaters, notably in Argentina
and Uruguay

"In the vast Plate system there swims a magnificent golden fish, the dorado, whose game qualities are little known to others in northern climes. Yet there are few fish so bold and gallant, or capable of giving an angler such a nerve-tingling battle. The fish is remarkable for its color, which is a soft gold shade, but still of a brilliance that is quite dazzling – something difficult to characterize and beautiful to see. Its scales are moderately large and of uniform hue, though there are some darker series of scales, running along the body in dotted stripes that lend additional vivacity to the basal tone. The fins of the fish are of a fine vermillion, except the tail, which has a black horizontal bar passing through its center. From this bar, the tail blends through gold in the middle to scarlet at the outer edges. The tail is emarginated in shape but is usually much worn away in mature specimens."

From Game Fish of the World *by Leander J. McCormick, 1949.*

Target weight: 30lbs
Dream weight: 50lbs
Areas: South America
Food: Fish and crustaceans

SUMMARY
Dorado prefer fast water and seek out rocks, submerged tree trunks, and any structure that gives them a break from the flow and good ambush possibilities.

There's an interesting paradox to the dorado that several anglers have mentioned to me. On the one hand, the fish is extraordinarily beautiful and sporting. The golden color is hard to forget. The fight is so dramatic aerially that you could be hooked into a tarpon. And yet, beneath this glamour, there is menace. A 30-inch fish will have a head almost a third of that length. The mouth is cavernous. It's armed with row upon row of short triangular teeth that are sharp, strong, and capable of inflicting the most tearing of wounds. In fact, those that use spinners and spoons often remark that the metal is deeply gouged by the power of the teeth and jaw. So, beautiful, yes, but the dorado is, at heart, a deadly hunter.

I could kick myself. Three times I've been all but on the plane to Argentina after dorado when life has intervened and I've had to cancel. Each time I've been devastated. Everyone tells me just how magnificent dorado are. I remember a day spent pike fishing with a neighbour, Nick Zoll, on a cold, winter's day when he extolled the virtues of these fabulous, golden, fighting fish. Shirley Deterding is another. You'll not find anything like the dorado, she's been telling me for years.

And now I've got Henry Gilbey on the phone telling me that his days after dorado were perhaps the most thrilling of his angling life. How bad do I feel now? Especially because if Henry tells you something you believe it. Henry is perhaps the foremost in a band of young adventurers, men like James Warbrick-Smith, Nick Hart, and Dave Lambert, guys who have given their life to their fishing, guys who will stop at nothing to fulfill their piscatorial dreams. I just love this hunger in them. Every conversation is fresh and exciting and makes you want to get out there, doing it still. So when I asked Henry to describe a typical day in his recent dorado expedition, I just drooled. I couldn't believe I hadn't been on that flight.

GOLDEN DORADO FACTS

• According to McCormick, there are four varieties of dorado – *salminus maxillosus*, *salminus brevidens*, *salminus hilarii,* and *salminus affinis*. *Maxillosus* is the prime sporting candidate however. Interestingly it is a member of the characin which is represented in Africa by the Goliath tiger fish. Am I ever going to get to grips with these gruesome cousins!?

March 2008. The Uruguay River, Uruguay. Henry Gilbey in conversation with John Bailey.

An average day, then, John. Right. We leave the estancia early, a comfortable lodge, good food and beds and drive some five minutes to the dam. Everything is tightly controlled. The guys check our passports, take the numbers, make us realize that fishing so close to a dam like this in Argentina is a hell of a privilege. As we're standing there we're aware that the river beneath the dam is going mental. There are fish, dorado, just ripping into small fry. Crazy. Ominous almost. It's scary. There are four of us in two boats, a brilliant arrangement because the river here, where it comes out of the dam, is big, seriously big. I'm not good on distances but it's got to be close on seven or eight hundred yards across, yes, getting on for a kilometer. Massive.

It's warm, cloudy though, perhaps with rain to come. We're not bothered. There are dorado everywhere. Absolute monsters are crashing on the surface. The landscape around isn't really pretty. You've got the dam for a kick off and the banks are more like marsh or drab grassland dotted with trees. But you don't care at all. Your whole attention, your whole focus is on those fish. I'm using a Greys Missionary 6, the 40 to 100 gram model. A 6000 model fixed spool reel. Fifty pound braid. The clutch is tightened right down. I've got a selection of spinners with me, poppers like Roosters and the Storm Chugbug. Some shallow divers that go to five feet or so. The Storm Thunderstick is great. And I've got a few Rapala Magnums to go down deeper than that. I've been told to replace all the trebles with 5/0s. Seems these dorado can just mash metal like nothing else. And it's true. We get out onto the river. It's almost like a salmon river I guess. Broad as I've said, deep in places, quite quick, moving swiftly over big rocks. You can't exactly see the dorado, the water's a bit too cloudy for that, but their movements are obvious everywhere as they're chasing prey fish. Sometimes they're on the surface hunting. Sometimes the water just boils. It's awesome. As I've said, there's something almost terrifying, primeval about it. These are big fish and they're just hunting, crazy for food.

You won't believe the surface action I'm experiencing. It's like the very best saltwater fishing I've had, only in fresh. The surface lures are just smashed. There's nothing technical about it. I'm casting where my guide tells me to and bang. Smack. It's absolutely crazy, devastating stuff. These dorado have to be like giant trevally. It's like they see the lure and they just glow, they bristle, they can't help mounting an attack. It's as though this crazed hunger takes them over, drives them insane. And what gets me is that they're hitting the lures almost the instant they hit the water. What I know is happening is that they're tracking the lures coming at them actually through the air itself. There's no way they could hit them so soon by sound of entry alone. God no. These fish are as predatorial as any I've ever come across. It's got me scared. I've just returned a 40 pounder and that's huge, really huge. I'm hardly bothering to photograph 20s. The guides are saying it's so great here because the water is low and it's unpressured. And also because there are thousands of prey fish here to attract them. There are dorado all over Argentina but there's nowhere quite like this. There's got to be a best place and I'm on it.

GRAYLING *Thymallus thymallus*

The Gracious Lady of the Stream

Region: Alaska, Northern Canada, and Europe

"Her pectoral and ventral fins were golden yellow, but the latter were marbled with brown over the gold, looking like the breast of a thrush caught in a shaft of sunlight. Her eye was ringed deep with gold. Most beautiful, her top three rows of scale, from her tip to her tail, caught now the light from the sky, then the reflection from the water and glistened in turn with shifting silvers, blues and purples. And most strange, on each flank, parallel to each other from the head to the ventral fin, ran two golden lines, as though traced in gold dust, by an angel."

From Travels with a Two-Piece *John Bailey 1985.*

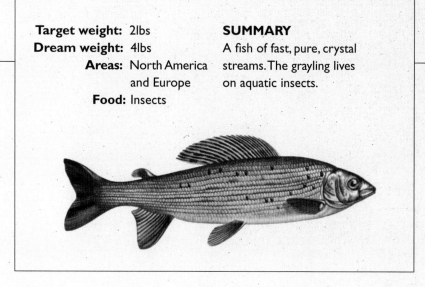

Target weight: 2lbs
Dream weight: 4lbs
Areas: North America and Europe
Food: Insects

SUMMARY
A fish of fast, pure, crystal streams. The grayling lives on aquatic insects.

Grayling are exclusively fish of cool, clear, streamy water. In fact, I've fished for grayling in nine countries and in something over 73 rivers and, do you know, I can't think of a single, solitary grayling run that hasn't been a scene of total beauty. Grayling are a beautiful fish – one of the most beautiful – and they just don't do places that don't reflect them, that don't do them justice.

Think of the Test, all quintessential English countryside. Water meadows. Weeping willows. Quiet villages and country pubs. You'll find them there. Think of Scotland's Tweed or Tay. Massive rivers, plunging through barren, desolate hillsides. Purple heather. Stags roaring in the autumn. There you'll find grayling. Think of rivers in Poland, Slovenia, Slovakia, and Austria. Meadows of wildflowers. Tyrolean-type villages. Crystal clear water. Mountains clustered around. There you will find grayling.

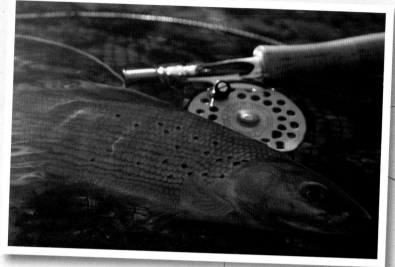

There are two things you should know about grayling. The first is that they have the most extraordinary eyesight, and this is enhanced by the invariably clear water in which they live. This means that if there's anything wrong whatsoever with the presentation of your bait or your fly, then they'll simply not be having it. Simple as that. The second thing you must be aware of is that even if they are taking whatever you put before them, they have the most discriminating of taste buds. If they sense a smidgen wrong with what they've consumed, then it's out of their mouth in a trillisecond. There is no faster fish in the world at ejecting the distasteful. Of course, this means that you're up against it. In the first place, you've going to find it very difficult to hoodwink a grayling and in the second place, you're going to have to have the reactions of a rattlesnake to turn the deception into a hooked up fish. You've been warned.

I used to think that there were only two ways to catch a grayling, and both are equally valid. The first way is with rod, center pin reel, float, and bait. This can be maggots, red worms or even sweetcorn! Picture this. It's a glorious autumn or winter day (grayling are always best pursued in cold weather) and you'll be on, necessarily, a gorgeous river. You'll probably be wading because it's good to get out there with the fish. The stream will just be strong enough to pull line off the center pin without you having to help it along. You'll mend the line and guide the float down its bobbing, weaving course. Then it dips. Perhaps the fish is 50 or 70 or even 100 yards away. Your strike sweeps back and clunk, you're into a big, twisting fish, shockingly strong for its size. The clue is in that massive dorsal fin. It's not a fin, it's a fan. If a two pounder gets that dorsal fin up against a brisk current, you're in for it. Brilliant. This isn't hanging on for dear life, a fight of brute force and ignorance. This is more exquisite, more guile than guts, more brain than brawn.

The second way to grayling fish, I always thought, is to pursue them with deep-presented nymphs. This, really, is the Czech nymphing style and it's deadly. Again you wade out and flick a team of two or three flies upstream, five yards or so. Then let them drift down opposite you and beneath before repeating the process. The flies are suspended by a small, polystyrene indicator. You just have to use one of these if you're going to see more than one bite in a million! In the right hands, this method is absolutely deadly. And it's great fun. You're so close to the fish. Sometimes you can actually see a grayling twist and take the nymph. If it's a big fish, two pounds or over, your strike won't rock him at all. He will sit there, simply shaking his head, totally disbelieving he could have made such an elementary mistake.

Yes, they are the two ways I always felt were the best to take grayling. Then, I met Jeremy Lucas.

GRAYLING FACTS

• For float fishing, an ideal rod is 13 or 14 feet in length with a crisp action. Three pound main line from reel to hook is perfect. For fly fishing, a-10 foot, four-weight rod provides lightness and complete control. Team this up with a light reel, floating line, and tippets of no more than two to three pounds breaking strain.

• For fly fishing, a 3-6 weight outfit is generally ideal, depending on the size of the fish, the river, and the force of the current.

May 2007. River San, Poland.

What a stunning river. Wide, shallow, crystal clear, festooned with grayling. I spend the day by the side of Jeremy Lucas, England fly fishing international, and it's been magical. He's been working upstream, sighting rising grayling and putting small dry flies to them, often at 25 to 30 yards range. Fish after fish has succumbed. It's like watching a wizard at work. His skill is in the accuracy of his casting and the delicacy of his presentation. Time after time, that fly goes down like thistledown an exact two feet above the rising fish and in exactly the right thread of water. And time after time, a neb comes up, a fly disappears, and a strike is successfully made.

But this is the best bit. A storm is coming in rapidly from the south. The evening sky has almost completely darkened over. There are rumbles of thunder, slivers of lightning, the first spots of approaching rain. Now, Jeremy and I are watching fish close to us, a rod length out, no more. And they're big, big Polish grayling. Many are two pounds, some, I swear, are three. Even four. And they're taking the tiniest of black

fly, nothing larger than midges really. And that's what Jeremy is pursuing them with. Size 20 gnats. Flies you can hardly see to thread on the line.

The fish are picky to a degree you couldn't believe. Again and again, they just hump under the fly. Jeremy is watching like a hawk. There's tension, concentration everywhere, in his face, in his shoulders, in the flicking of his rod, rapier-like against the black clouds.

And, hear it, there's a quite audible slurp. The fish is on. It's cartwheeling. It's huge. The fish is netted, adored and released and now the rain is coming down in stair rods. We run to the shelter of a barn, both laughing, both ecstatic. Thank God for the gift of grayling.

ATLANTIC SALMON *Salmo salar*

Unparalleled Spirit

Region: Europe and Russia from the Artic to northern Spain.
North America's northeast coast

"Deep down we all want to catch a real, silver, Atlantic salmon despite whatever we might say. There isn't an angler anywhere in the world who doesn't want one of these boys if they're dead honest with themselves. Guys like me genuinely love all the species we have in our own country but I'm here because there's one fish I just gotta catch before I go. I guess my life just wouldn't be complete without one."

US visitor and angler at Blackwater Lodge, Southern Ireland, in conversation with John Bailey, June 2002.

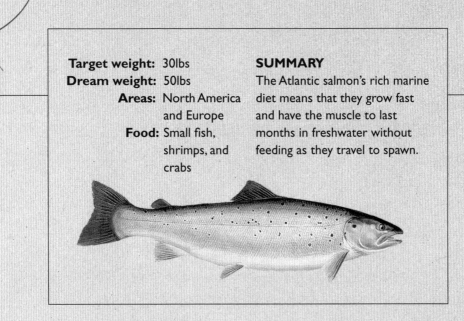

Target weight: 30lbs
Dream weight: 50lbs
Areas: North America and Europe
Food: Small fish, shrimps, and crabs

SUMMARY
The Atlantic salmon's rich marine diet means that they grow fast and have the muscle to last months in freshwater without feeding as they travel to spawn.

Yes. My friend said it all. There's just something so evocative about the salmon, its beauty, its iconic status, its planetary wanderings. But, for me, it gets into the 50 because of one word. Power. Two words perhaps. Unquenchable power. We all know the fantastic biological story of the salmon. How it spends most of its adult life in the ocean, navigating back to the river of its birth, desperate to spawn on the redds where its own life began. Whatever the cost, whatever the effort, the salmon must return.

All this is good in theory. In practice, it's even more dramatic. It's October up in Glen Garry. Salmon have been netted at the fish traps and now they are in huge holding tanks waiting to be stripped of their eggs and milt and for the resulting fingerlings to be artificially reared.

It's very early in the morning. As I walk down towards the tanks, I can hear an almost volcanic splashing. The tanks are large, the size of a small room perhaps, and they're filled by six inch pipes which feed solid plumes of water to the fish. There's one cock salmon that you can't fail but notice. He weighs possibly 20 pounds and he's colored deep red. His jaw is hooked, his eyes defiant. But what is so remarkable is that for the half an hour I watch him, he constantly forces

himself through that jet of water. The pressure of that water is astounding – I can't hold my own hand steady in it such is its force. And yet, in his deep-rooted desire to reach his objective, that salmon forces himself again and again to the limits of his endurance. There is something so nobly tragic about the scene that, at last, I must tear myself away.

It's a similar level of power that I witnessed again on northeast Canada's Miramichi river in 2007. Tim, within 15 minutes of arriving on the bankside, hooks into a colossal salmon. He fights it for 15 minutes exactly. I'd like to say the fish jumped 15 times, too, but I'm not sure on that one. It certainly spends a lot of time airborne, certainly enough for us to realize here is a fish of well over 40 pounds in weight. Tim's a good angler. His gear is sound. He's piling on the pressure. And yet, that fish is never remotely subdued. From the start of the battle to its sad finish, the salmon always has the upper hand. Tim knows it. He's not really surprised when the fish eventually wakes, runs irresistibly, and breaks free. It is, of course, the largest salmon he has ever hooked. He'll probably never hook a larger one. Just to be attached is sensational enough. Of course, though, it doesn't help for the rest of the week when we bump into endless Canadian anglers who tells us a story of the English guy who lost a whopper.

The day after Tim lost his fish, the wind was hellish. The temperatures had plummeted, just to be on the bank was an ordeal. In truth, I didn't fancy fishing at all then, slowly, it dawned on me. In all my fishing life, I'd never been so close to so many huge Atlantic salmon. I guess in a single 20-minute span, I counted a dozen different fish all over 30 pounds in weight. My God, I thought, what am I doing sitting here?

For two hours I fished like a Dervish. Fishing on a Bomber – a big, floating fly – I had three fish come to inspect, rolling over the fly, rocking it, always refusing. One of those fish weighed 40 pounds. I had another monster swirl over a shrimp pattern and another that even nipped the fly, was hooked an instant and then just powered – that word again – off into the dark river.

By lunch, I was exhausted, played out. Throughout the 1980s, I had spent my life and my fortune trying to catch a 30 pound salmon. I doubt whether I was even ever close.

Perhaps on a couple of occasions, I and my 30 pounder were together on a river. And here, in a single morning, I'd lived my dream of monsters. That's how salmon fishing is. At its very best, it's fishing taken to a whole new level, to a state of exhilaration impossible to describe.

ATLANTIC SALMON FACTS

• The world is against the wild salmon. There's netting at sea. There's still netting on many estuaries despite many of the nets-men being bought off. Fish cages are calamitous. The sea lice problem is immense – for sea trout even more than salmon. There's always the problem of escapees mingling with the stocks of the wild fish. There's disease. There's global warming. There's the general degradation of the seas.

September 1984. The Barle, Somerset, England.

The Tarr Steps is a hotel still, run in its legendary eccentric way by Desmond. It's been raining for two days. The river is full, colored and steadying. The grilse, those delightful, small, sleek salmon are running in big numbers. I spent last evening looking at the pools, planning an attack. Now, my alarm clock is ringing. There's just a little light coming through the curtains and I'm away up the river.

I'm heading to the Hinds Leap Pool, below the old bridge. It's a deeper, more placid pool than most and I reckon plenty of fish will hold up especially on the bank where the stream comes in and the alders overhang. The walk is full of mystery. The Barle valley is narrow and steep and the trees drip rain. There are columns of mist. The air is warm, close, choking. If ever a river were haunted...

You break out into more open fields. The light is growing. I've been walking perhaps 20 minutes and the pool I'm seeking isn't far ahead. As I arrive, it's a case of wow, look at that! A grilse of six or seven pounds tops in mid-river, frozen on the surface a second, its tail then splashing goodbye.

I'm fishing a single-handed outfit, a seven weight with a floating line. I wade out as far as I safely can and put the fly across to the alders to let it swing around in the current. It's black, about an inch and a half long with a single hook, barb removed. Third cast there's a gleam a foot beneath the surface and my fly line slowly pulls itself straight. I lift into the fish. The water erupts. There's one dangerous moment when the fish threatens to get out of the pool and make for the rapids beneath. I pile on the pressure and turn him and shortly afterwards release him. Even today, I don't know what made me slip that fish back. But there was a voice, somewhere in my head, asking whether I needed him either for the table or, come to that, for my ego.

To see the silver fish slide back into another new morning was a more precious morning, all I needed to take from the river.

PACIFIC SALMON *Oncorhynchus tshawytscha*

The King of Fish

Region: North America – Alaska to California. North-east Asia

"Hope you're not going to get all sniffy on me boy, start looking down that long nose at me. I've had you English guys out here before getting all picky over our salmon just because they ain't Atlantics. But you're on the west coast now, not the east and I'm telling you these are some of the damndest fine salmon in the world boy."

Big Bob, British Columbia Guide in conversation with the author, 1996.

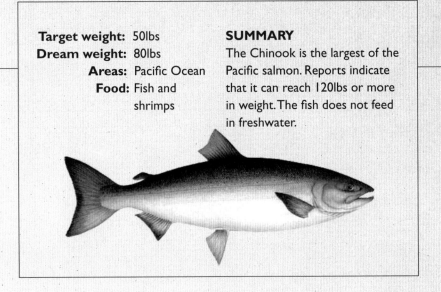

Target weight: 50lbs
Dream weight: 80lbs
Areas: Pacific Ocean
Food: Fish and shrimps

SUMMARY
The Chinook is the largest of the Pacific salmon. Reports indicate that it can reach 120lbs or more in weight. The fish does not feed in freshwater.

The bond between man and Pacific salmon has always been elemental. One of my favorite pieces in angling literature is from *Going Fishing* by Negley Farson. He describes the 1913 catastrophe on the Fraser River when the "Big Run" of sockeye salmon was destroyed. "But when they were building the Canadian Northern Railway's tunnel at Yale in 1913, an engineer underestimated the strength of a blast he had ordered. Instead of breaking loose merely a calculated cubic quantity of rock, it knocked the entire face of the cliff into the river.

"It was a sight to make a man scream," said McPherson. "I watched thousands and thousands of salmon have a try at that leap. Men worked like beavers to help the fish past. We built fish ladders on the side flumes; we hauled away boulders by sheer sweat alone. I tore the nails off me hands. We were frenzied, you know — we knew what it meant, if that Big Run did not get past. But it was no use. Millions and millions of fish died at the foot of the water shooting over those fallen rocks. They couldn't make it. Nine feet — the fish made the height — but they couldn't face the fire hose. That's what it was like. Your heart broke when you saw that water hit them and hurl them back. With their eggs still inside them, they died — and with them died the Big Run of Fraser."

It's always been one of my unrequited wishes to see a run of sockeye salmon when they are in their spawning crimsons. I've seen photographs. Rivers carpeted bank to bank with a blood-red swarm. Watching Atlantics head to their spawning grounds can be awesome but, I guess, nothing compares with this. This is nature at her most fundamentally compelling.

Big Bob was right. We caught a coho that was absolutely as silver as its secondary name suggests. Bob informed me that it was just from the sea and it absolutely glistened. Perhaps it weighed 10 pounds or so, but that's really not the point. It was a wonderful fish that fought with just the power of any Atlantic I've tangled with. There were a lot more fish about that morning and I could have made a real killing. I chose not to only because all the fish seemed of similar size and having caught one I sort of felt I'd done it. To this day, I can't decide whether Big Bob respected or ridiculed the decision. That's so often the way with guides around the world. Sometimes there's simply the language problem which makes any meaningful conversation hard. There's frequently the issue of the tip. If a guide thinks being outspoken is going to lose him hard cash, well, with a family to feed, he buttons it. To others, guiding is just a job, a way of filling in the hours profitably, and they don't really give a damn what a client does, says, or how he acts. They've got more on in their lives than to worry. But having said all that, there are many guides like Big Bob. Men who just like to assess you, weigh you up, make their own private decision on you. When I was younger, I used to find this type of treatment unnerving. This wears off as you get older. You know more about who you are

and you get a better idea of your own worth – or lack of it – as the years go by.

I suppose of all the five strains of Pacific salmon, the one to make it indisputably into the 50 would be the King or Chinook salmon. They are impossibly big. Perhaps it's this massive size of theirs that has meant some European sportsmen haven't quite taken them seriously. When they get into freshwater, they tend to color up quickly and lose that distinctive, graceful shape of the salmon family. A common local name for a very big King is "Hog". An injustice but perhaps that's how some sports anglers who should have known better have viewed them in the past. In truth, a big King salmon is a glorious prize. They can be difficult to fool and they can be even more difficult to land…

PACIFIC SALMON FACTS

• The smaller chum and pink salmon are less regarded as game fish but have important commercial value. Sockeye salmon grow well into double figures but it's the Kings and the coho that are the most important sporting varieties. Cohos (or silvers) can exceed 30 pounds and come upriver in large numbers. Chinooks (or Kings) are considered large at 40 or 50 but 60s, 70s, and even 80s and 90s are there to be caught.

2008. An unnamed river in Alaska. Shirley Deterding in conversation with the John Bailey.

Scott, the guide, woke me up long, long before dawn. This was the plan. He'd told me the night before that if I wanted to hook into a serious King, a monster, it was important to get out on the pool before any of the others, to fish it with the first of the coming light. He said that so many times people underestimate Kings. They might be big, but they're not stupid. Treat them with the respect you would any fish and you will get the best of them. And so it was.

The forest was dark and quiet. There were none of the usual fish eagles in the sky. The squirrels were still holed up. Scott told me to keep my eyes open for bear. It seemed that this was a tricky time of the day for them. I was fishing a 10-weight, I remember. A fast-sink line. A big fly but I can't tell you what it was now. Our plan was to cast across the river a long way and put in a big mend as the line and the fly were going down. Then, when everything was in line and set, a slow, twitchy retrieve.

The pool was a long one and we worked down it slowly, very carefully, Scott telling me not to rush. "No panic," he kept saying. "There's nobody about. We've got everything on our side." He made me realize that Kings swim either alone or in very small groups. They're not like coho that come up in great numbers so you've got to search the water meticulously to find them. I'd had 40, maybe 50 casts. I can't tell you now, but suddenly the line went solid, dead, like I'd hit into a log. There were just a few seconds of complete indecision when that log began to move very, very fast.

I've said fast. Unstoppable is much more like it. I've hit big fish before in the sea and on Atlantic salmon rivers but this thing was in a league of its own. I don't know how many minutes I'd been playing it when it came up and thrashed on the surface. Scott simply muttered, "Holy shit" I remember the words with complete precision and then he added, "That mother is 70 plus!" If I hadn't been scared before, I was then.

The light grew. The fish kept going. We passed the rod from one to the other. My strength just wasn't up to it and Scott said later neither would his have been. In the end, we followed it all the way to the estuary. Don't ask me exactly, but it was well over a mile that fish took us. I guess we'd never been closer to the fish than 50 or 60 yards and it was still ploughing on and on, the sea firmly on its mind. How long a fight? I'd say definitely we were well into the second hour by now. Scott said we'd just have to make a stand to try and stop it. So we did. The line had long gone and now did most of the backing. We kept clamping down on the reel, tightening the clutch but more and more backing went with sickening, juddering spurts. And then there was nothing. I reeled and I reeled and eventually got the lot back. The hook had come out, pulled straight. We just looked at each other and shrugged. Hey, I thought, that was a plan that worked. Almost.

FEROX TROUT *Salmo trutta ferox*

The Giant Trout of the Glacial Lakes

Region: The glacial lakes of North, West and Central Europe, including Iceland

"I clicked on the spool and wound down to the disappearing line. Everything grew tight and I hit the fish with all the might of the rod in my hands. For that second I believed it was the bouldered bottom again but when the line zipped through the waves at the stern of the boat and off into the waste waters at the Mansion loch I knew that ferox, like lightning, had struck this once. Very soon affairs were desperate. I had never felt a fish of this power and this manner of fight before. The runs, even though the fish was deep, were breathtaking, forcing me to follow into the swell. Soon I was motoring after the fish – trying to keep the line tight, trying to steer the boat and keep a proper speed behind the ferox."

From **In Wild Waters** *John Bailey, 1989.*

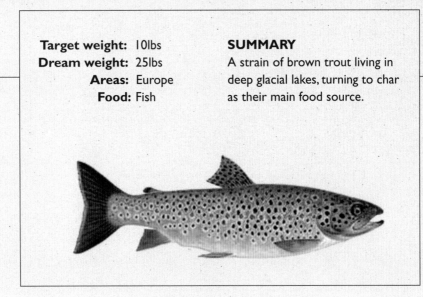

Target weight: 10lbs
Dream weight: 25lbs
Areas: Europe
Food: Fish

SUMMARY
A strain of brown trout living in deep glacial lakes, turning to char as their main food source.

Ferox. The massive predatorial brown trout of glacial lakes. Ferox. Ferocious. The name says it all. There's history attached to the ferox, first identified by the Victorian sportsmen as they pushed north through Scotland fishing and shooting as they went. Here, in the cold, massively deep lochs they contacted huge browns, routinely 10, sometimes 20, and culminating in an extraordinary one time record of 39 pounds. There wasn't a chalkstream in the world that could produce monsters like this.

The key to the success of the ferox lies with the Arctic char that became landlocked in these waters with the retreat of the Ice Cap 10,000 years ago. These fish average 4 to 12 ounces in weight – a perfect bite size for a ferox – and shoal up in vast numbers – an unmissable target for a species not naturally suited to predatory work like the pike. At times, generally dawn and dusk, lucky anglers witness the phenomenal sight of ferox hunting char in the surface zone. Char lift out as numerous as raindrops, as the huge trout charge among them. The fury might last four or five minutes before the loch settles back into its usual inscrutable self.

The majority of feroxing is done on the troll, trailing two or three lures behind a slowly moving boat. The baits can be artificial spoons and plugs or dead char attached to trebles so that they revolve and wobble as they move through the water. Ferox tend to hunt between 5 and 20 feet down so that's where you work your lures. And ferox keep on the fin, too – always following the strong subsurface currents, hoping to come across bodies of char in their wanderings. For this reason, the troller keeps on the move, the engine ticking over slowly, hour after uneventful hour.

Fly anglers call this dull stuff but there's an art to it, especially during the elemental storms that can sweep waters as large and exposed as these. To be caught in a column of spin drift as your boat is pummelled by a force eight northerly is an experience you don't forget. And, then when a lure is hammered and the rod wrenches in the rest, reel shrieking, line hissing to the dark water, the hours of boredom are quickly forgotten.

There are times, too, when ferox can be caught on the fly, one occasion I'll soon be recounting. Generally, though, ferox can be fly-caught in the autumn when they drift from the lochs into the rivers where they spawn. Here, they become hugely territorial as they defend their redds and they will pursue any large streamer fly to destruction. Imagine. Snow on the mountain tops. The stags roaring as the rut intensifies. The splendid deepening colors of the hills. The yard of leopard-flecked brown trout hurtling down the white water in search of the loch, its refuge. It doesn't happen often but when it does it's like the strike of a fish thunderbolt. But that is the essence of feroxing: endless periods of waiting punctuated by the most adrenaline pumping moments a man can imagine.

Ireland's loughs Corrib and Mask have seen some of my best feroxing days. The lochs of Wester Ross and Invernesshire have come very close, but it's an exceptional two hours in Iceland that tells you so much about these fabulous trout.

FEROX TROUT FACTS

• Normal brown trout in glacial lochs peak at three years and die around six years. Ferox turn predatorial around three to four years of age and then grow for a further seven to 10 years reaching a large size and an old age. Ferox also spawn with ferox to maintain the integrity of the strain. Ferox range through the glacial lakes of England, Wales, Ireland, Scotland, Scandinavia, Iceland, and Central Europe.

May, 2005 Arni's Lake in southern Iceland.

Ferox don't do boring landscapes. Wherever you find them there is geological drama and Iceland doesn't fail in this. This is the land of unfolding and unremitting wonderment. Imagine the sun rolling around the midnight horizon. Glaciers glittering on the rim of the mountains to the east. A landscape without cars, rarely with a village. A gleam always in the sky with pillars of light shafting down unexpectedly from cracks in the clouds, reflecting off the snow-capped hills. Here, there's a volcano, a ridiculously perfect pyramid, jet black against the blaze of sunset. Jets of steam disappear towards the just visible stars. This is what I see as Geiri, our guide, pulls down a track towards a vast lake that lies before us to the south. We pull in by the side of a large bay which swarms with fish, with char mostly and smaller brown trout. The water's surface is pockmarked by their rings as they rise for midges in the mild evening half-light. But, every now and again, there is an eruption and char shower out before a hunter. There are ferox about.

Geiri's reel is screaming. We run to the sound. The fly line is gone. The backing is steaming out into the depths. The battle lasts 35 minutes and then a double figured ferox comes to the shallows. This is an awesome fish to be caught on a small fly but the night holds one more bombshell. By now it's closing on midnight but it's still bright enough to see deep into the bay. I'm bringing in a nice char of a pound when, from the deep dark water beneath, a trout like a leopard charges it. It turns away. It comes back. Its gills flare. My char is gone. So, with a wrench of the line, is the ferox. Twenty-five pounds is my guess.

I haven't been back to that lake since that night but it's always in my dreams, always in my plans? Perhaps there are adventures best left forever in the imagination.

SEA TROUT _Salmo trutta_

See Them Shine

Region: Eastern Atlantic rivers, North Sea rivers, rivers where th
are brown trout – notably South America

_"All fish are pearls of nature" says Hugh Falkus to me. "But sea trout are so quick,
so secretive. Here today, gone tomorrow under cover of night. The silver fish. See
them shine under a moon. That's why, of all fish, they've so dominated my life."_

_Conversation with Hugh Falkus, August 1989, Crag Cottage,
Lake District, England._

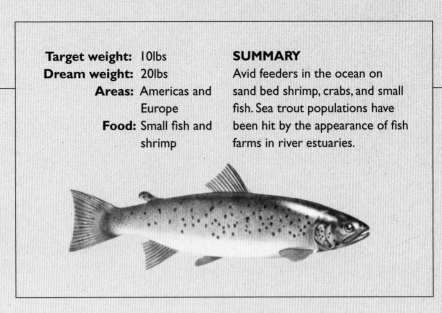

Target weight: 10lbs
Dream weight: 20lbs
Areas: Americas and Europe
Food: Small fish and shrimp

SUMMARY
Avid feeders in the ocean on sand bed shrimp, crabs, and small fish. Sea trout populations have been hit by the appearance of fish farms in river estuaries.

Sea trout are basically browns that decide to set off for the salt. It's something like the relationship of rainbows and steelhead. And, just like the steelhead, the sea trout seem to possess that added vitality that the oceans give. And, whilst a brow trout defends its lie lifelong, a sea trout is a wanderer, a nomad, the scope of their world immense.

That's why the sea trout makes the 50. It's this will of the wisp nature. As Hugh said, memorably, here today, gone tomorrow, you can never rely on sea trout. And, like any transitory relationship, the moments you have with sea trout are indescribably magical.

Between 1969 and 1976 I was obsessed with them, May until September. This was the period of my gap year, my university years, my bum around years. Once work got me then sea trouting was just no use. To be a successful sea trouter you live for them alone. Nothing else – certainly not work - can be allowed to exist. Certainly not around the coast of Norfolk. There are many places like this around the shorelines of northern Europe. There are places where no sea trouting rules exist. There are no named pools. There are no highly prized beats. These are the sort of places fished by locals, by those in the know, by those who have built up huge banks of experience. After seven years, I could just about predict, if I were lucky, where sea trout would be about one tide in five. If I were really on my game perhaps it would be one tide in three. These could be massive fish. I saw a photograph once of a 23 pounder. I know it wasn't a salmon. I saw a fish one August cruise under an old stone bridge that was at least as large. And I had plenty myself between eight and 11 or so pounds. My monster, though, always eluded me. Just…

There was one night. It was a dreary, drizzly sort of evening. Very cold, I remember. A north wind coming in off the sea, across the desolate marshes numbing my fingers. I'd known a big fish was on the bend for two days past. I'd seen it – glimpsed it rather – and plotted its downfall. It took me at a rush, and I knew it was massive. You've got to remember this is a long while back, and I'm not exactly sure how long the battle lasted. I know I followed the fish for just short of a mile – I walked that stretch of river bank only a couple of days back, so I'm absolutely sure on that one. The river's not as deep now or as wide, and the flow has dwindled massively, so I doubt if huge fish will ever make their way up it again. That saddens me. The loss of that fish, that gloomy night, saddened me, too. I suppose, with hindsight, I'd hung on just so long that I felt luck was with me and I'd get my prize. You know how it is. The longer a fight lasts, the more you feel the gods are with you and the more you sense the tide swinging your way. In fact, I probably would have got that fish had it not been for the sluice gate, that dreadful, iron, unforgiving barrier between the freshwater and the sea. When the fish got through that, my dreams were over. Simple as that. I retired to the pub, and not for the first time in my life got drunk over the loss of a fish.

So that was the biggest sea trout that I personally have ever been in contact with. There have, in the past, been occasional opportunities for me to pursue big sea trout in Sweden, Patagonia and, especially, in Argentina. I've got mates who've taken 20 pounders down there and shown me photographs that make me gawp. But, you know, there's just something about that style of fishing that doesn't grab me. I suppose if I ever do have my monster, I want it to be on my own terms, somewhere in the wilderness, somewhere no one would ever expect. A bit like North Uist.

SEAT TROUT FACTS

• Traditionally, sea trout fishing is best at night. Or so they've always said! In actual fact, sea trout can be stalked and caught during the day. Frequently, though, you've got to go lighter. Small dry flies work. Even as tiny as a 14 or a 16. You've got to be incredibly cautious. You can't afford any mistakes. It's all tight, all neat, and it can be hugely exciting and successful.

June 2001, Hebrides, Scotland.

Christopher had always told me that I would love the Hebridean sea pools and he's right. I can scarcely believe the scale, the desolation, the colors, the sheer beauty of what I'm looking at now. The sand seems to reach forever, certainly until it meets the sea and the sea is so far I can barely make it out, I definitely can't hear it. The tide is low and still receding and that, says Christopher, gives us our best chance. Maddy, the world's best dog, is going wild as ever chasing seagulls with carefree abandon around this echoing world. Christopher has already lost a fish. He says it was big. I believe him. I watched his rod bend frighteningly, I could hear his reel 200 yards away. He followed it, I guess, 100 yards and then stomped back, swearing.

Now, I'm on one of the sea pools Christopher talks about. It's not really a pool, more a depression. Perhaps it's 20 yards across, 50 yards long and four or five feet deep. There's weed spraying in the current. The water is crystal clear. I look down at my feet where I'm wading in thigh-deep water and I see shrimp, small flatfish, crabs and even tiny bass a couple of inches long. It's a remarkable experience. Some of the sea trout jumping are big. I'm excited. I know, after a gap of a quarter of a century, I'm close to my dream of a big one.

It's not big but it's furious. Landed, lying in the kelp, admired hugely, I guess my North Uist sea trout weighs four pounds. Like Hugh said years back, this IS a pearl of nature. Even Maddy lets up a few minutes to come over and inspect. There's a moment of debate as to whether we should take the fish for supper. Christopher is a wondrous cook but I can't do it. The fish goes back. There's a little puff of sand where it was. There's a bow wave where it's going.

PERMIT

Trachinotus falcatus

Always Moving

Region: Europe, Asia, Scandinavia

"Most people have never heard of a permit, much less caught one. They are one of the prizes of flats' fishing and are a particularly difficult species to locate and catch. Permit are not as abundant as bonefish and they never seem to stop moving. If you think the grey ghost is skittish, try fishing for permit. They are seldom around long enough for a good presentation. When you have a shot, you must be on target or the fish are gone. Often a guide will point to a departing fish and announce, 'That was a permit'."

Fishing the Flats *Mark Sosin and Lefty Kreh*, 1983.

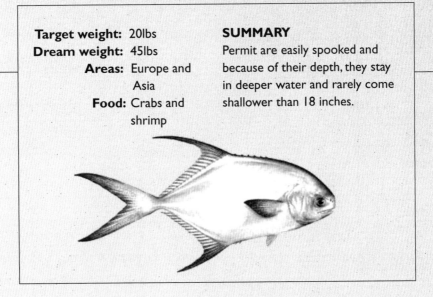

Target weight:	20lbs	
Dream weight:	45lbs	
Areas:	Europe and Asia	
Food:	Crabs and shrimp	

SUMMARY

Permit are easily spooked and because of their depth, they stay in deeper water and rarely come shallower than 18 inches.

Two of the greatest saltwater fly anglers in history are right. I, for example, had barely heard of a permit by the late 90s. A few rumors and whisperings. That was about it. Then along comes an English Game Fair and I'm asked to chair a panel of international experts on their fishing ambitions. I ask them all what they'd like to catch most in life and why. The usual culprits. Big marlin. Tarpon. A record this or a record that. Yawn-yawn, heard it all before. I come to Matt Hayes, one hell of a traveler, writer and presenter. "There's no doubt at all in my mind," he says.

"John, it's got to be a permit. And a permit on the fly, as well, come to that. And why? If you ask me, they're just about the biggest challenge you are ever going to come across in this fishing world. If you see one, you've done well. If you hook one, you've done better. If you land one, you're a mini-god." An American called from the back of the hall. Seems he's from Florida and fishes the Bahamas. He reckons Matt has got the subject nailed. He says he's landed one. An 18 pounder, too. Says he was walking on air for a whole month afterwards. Didn't have to buy a drink for six months. Voted Angler of the Year election time.

And then I ask for a vote in the marquee. About 150 anglers listening I guess. How many of them have heard of permit, I ask? About 10 put up their hands. How many have actually seen or caught, or even tried to catch a permit? Our American friend's hand shoots up. His alone. I make it my business to at least find out what all this permit stuff is all about.

PERMIT FACTS

• Permit are found in the warm, temperate and tropical west Atlantic primarily. They swim either singly or in small groups. To find one is hard; to hook one is harder and to land one is very difficult indeed. In large part, this is to do with the speed of the permit and its stamina. A bonefish can swim at a maximum of between 25 and 30 miles an hour. A blue fin tuna can hit speeds in excess of 40 miles an hour. The permit is somewhere between the two.

Letter to Phil Humm from John Bailey in the Bahamas, 2001.

No Phil, before you die of suspense, I haven't succeeded. Not quite anyway. But I'm happy with what I achieved out there and I'll tell you for why. What was made quite clear to me by the guides is that you're not likely to see bones and permit in the same areas. Seems the bones can tolerate much shallower water than permit which are much deeper in the flank. There are more bones. They're more visible. They don't move quite as far and fast. So you've got to look for permit in a totally different way. And that probably means missing out on the bones.

So okay, that's what I did. Day after day I spend my time just off the shallows, walking the drop-offs. Looking into water between three and six feet deep. Hardly a hardship mate. I saw just about every fish that swims the western Atlantic. And caught a few too that I just couldn't resist putting a fly to. But I wasn't seeing any permit. Back to the guides again. So they reckoned that permit are even harder to see than bones. The scales just reflect the light in a way that makes them almost invisible. If you're lucky, all you're going to see is a bit of black on the dorsal or tail fin. The trick is to get into the zone. (Whatever that means!) To sort of go with the flow. To take in all the water in front of you without focusing unduly until you think you're given a clue. Perhaps it's the vague, blurred indistinct outline of a fish. Perhaps it's that flash of black they're talking about. Whatever, once you think a permit is in your range of vision, then you can focus hard, concentrate right on the area until you make out the fish itself.

That's exactly how it happened, Phil, on the fourth day of looking. There, two rod lengths from me, was my first sighted permit. I'm not even going to guess a weight. Fifteen pounds minimum. Thirty pounds maximum. One of those moments that the blood drains totally from your brain. I'm all fingers and thumbs. I can barely get a cast out at all. The fly goes in and the permit's away. I watch him go 20 yards, getting deeper all the time and that's it. My chance blown.

I'm writing you this because I know you'll understand. Of course, I'd have liked to have hooked the fish and even landed it but that you'll know how great that minute of excitement was. Okay, of course, the guides thought I'd really mucked up. I'd cast too short. Too long. Too close. Not close enough. One would have done it this way, another that way. There was endless debate over endless beers and I didn't give a monkey's. I sort of formed a plan, carried it out and, to a degree, and to my own satisfaction, it had worked. I reckon I'm one of the few Brits who's actually seen one of the damned things and at the moment, at this stage in my life, that's quite enough for me.

CONCLUSION

THE PERFECT FISH

CONCLUSION

"A beautiful, slate backed, silver flanked, pink finned, jewel encrusted, six inch roach."

Peter Lapsley describing his first fish caught on his sixth birthday in June 1949.

I hope Peter doesn't mind me using these few words that appeared first in the Salmon and Trout Association's magazine. I think they're important. I think they show that even one of the world's most famous fly anglers can still appreciate a humble roach, supposedly one of the journeymen of European fish species. Rubbish. They're not. If there's one message I would like this book to put across it is that all fish are equal and all fish are fantastic. In the end, YOUR 50 Fish are the ones that turn YOU on.

Of course, your main criteria could be size. I understand that. Catching a big fish is seductive. The trophy fish shot. The smile of triumph. A long journey perhaps well rewarded. A carving or a model of the fish for that space above the hearth. Your ego satisfied. The thrill of the battle always coursing in your veins. Marlin. Sturgeon. Huge catfish. The lure of the monster will always be a part of fishing. Yet, like Peter Lapsley, remember when you're small and even a small-finned thing was large? Truly, in my role as a guide, I've seen grown men become blabber-mouthed with excitement over fish just a few inches long. Size, as they say, isn't everything.

Perhaps it's all down to beauty? But beauty is very much in the eye of the beholder and a totally subjective matter. What is beauty to one angler is certainly not so to another. Take an Indian murrell. Some anglers who catch one simply see an ugly, sausage roll shaped, flat headed, angry eyed creature. Others look at the electrically vivid blue spotting patterns and the majesty of that mahogany sheen to the scales. It's the color combination found nowhere else on the planet. And think how mother murrell guard their young for months until they are big enough to fend for themselves. Watch the adult shepherd the baby in the margins of the river and you will appreciate more about this fascinating species. But they're all beautiful and interesting. In America, for example, I've seen men delighted with a bag of blue gill, crappies, pumpkin seed, and sunfish. I'm overjoyed when I catch a crucian carp – that little handsome puddle of gold.

Of course, it could be the place where you catch your fish that is paramount. Perhaps it's a vast glacial loch nestling in the backdrop of snow-capped mountains that thrills you. Or an isolated river winding its way over an enormous plain with skies above simply endless. Or it's a twinkling stream in the mountains or a chalk based river winding through the most fertile of meadows. Could be, though, you find your own particular peace on the village pond, no deeper than the average duck.

The company you fish with, of course, is vital and if it's good, it enhances every catch. I truly don't think there's a more civilized way of fishing than rod sharing with a friend. Admiring each other's skill. Joking at each other's failings and frustrations. Pride in a shared catch. A day made unforgettable by companionship.

The method that you use is important to many. An upstream nymph or dry fly is exquisite. Flicking a tiny spinner for a bass under the overhanging branches is mesmerizing. Casting to permit on the flats is as exciting and skillful and heart-in-the-mouth as it comes. But there are many who are happy lying asleep in a tent waiting for a carp to hook itself and for an electric bite alarm to tear up the serenity of the night. In the end, it's each to his own. The 50 Fish are the ones that populate your dreams, your desires.

INDEX

Page numbers in **bold** indicate main entry

ACKNOWLEDGMENTS
& CONTACTS

Acknowledgments

There are just so many people to thank at this stage in the history of the 50. As televisions shows are so fond of saying today, in no particular order...

Thank you to David Miller and Mick Loates for their magnificent and inspiring art work. To my mind, an illustration can speak volumes more than the simple photograph. Both of them have managed superbly to inject the soul and spirit into these wonderful fish.

Can I also thank the team of young, exciting, dynamic travelers that have helped me so much? Dave Lambert, Akshay Malavi, Neill Stephen, and Henry Gilbey have all been founts of wisdom beyond their years! I love their energy and their commitment. Simon Channing is totally special. Ten years ago, he was taking the adventure fishing world apart. He was one of my dearest traveling companions. I can't begin to recount all the fun and thrills that we shared. One day, more of his remarkable story will be told.

Older friends, too, have had their say. I will always be in the debt of Shirley Deterding, my near neighbor in Norfolk. Whether any woman has ever done more in the world of extreme angling, I seriously doubt. Shirley has always been an unquenchable spirit. And so she will always remain. Keith Elliott is one of my greatest friends. Cerebral, amusing, generous, utterly unselfish...a joy to be with either in the UK or the foothills of the Himalayas.

James Ellis – jungle Jim – was my neighbor for ten years and hardly a day went past without some conversation of excitement on the subject of field sports around the world. James has done it all. If the adventure isn't really terrifying, you can see his lack of interest! But when it comes to all the travelers, perhaps none of them is as dear to me as Johnny Jensen, my Great Dane from Denmark with whom I've shared so much over the years. India. Greenland. Russia. Kazakhstan. Sweden. On and on. Johnny lifts any trip to make it extraordinary.

And thank you Chris Tarrant for your generous preface. Few people realize just what a great and keen fisherman Chris is. It's a good job for the fish around the world that TV keeps him so busy, or they'd stand no chance. Make no mistake, Chris, apart from being the nicest of men, is one of the great anglers.

I'd like to give Matt Lowing of Carlton Books a big thank you. It was his imagination that let the book come to life. Many of the ideas are Matt's. Much of the direction of the book belongs to Matt. I've worked with many editors in the past but none nearly as sympathetic.

And finally, as ever, may I thank Carol Selwyn, my most treasured personal assistant without whom I would have achieved absolutely zero this past ten years.

Contacts

To accomplish the 50 you're going to need help. May I suggest Angling Travel (www.angling-travel.com) for advice on India, Greenland, Spain, and Mongolia, to name just a few areas where the company is active.

Fisherman's Valley (www.fishermansvalley.co.uk) should be able to help with many bait fish conundrums. Fisherman's Valley is also strong in Poland and in the search for huchen.

Akshay Malavi's website (www.gamefishingindia.com) should certainly be visited if you're going to sample the multitudinous delights of warm ocean sport fishing. The species Akshay can put you on are innumerable. And unnervingly exciting.

Dave Gibson over in Florida (dgibson@peganet.com) is perhaps the most colorful and engaging guide I've personally sailed with. What he doesn't know about tarpon really isn't worth knowing anyway.

Jeremy Lucas (www.wilderness-flyfishing.co.uk) is your expert in Poland. And if you just want a gentle day out on the River Thames, fishing from a punt for innumerable species in gracious company, then may I recommend Roger Wyndham Barnes? Contact him on +44 (0) 118 9342 981 for The Thames Experience. Justin Anwyl could be your man for the UK sea bass experience. (www.bass-fishing.co.uk)

Finally, it's worth keeping a very close eye on the Hardy and Greys website magazine Fin and Fly. (www.hardygreys.com) Every month there are stories and reports of fishing around the world that will inspire and inform. This great company has the widest network of contacts, so make sure you plug in to the nerve center of sport fishing.

ILLUSTRATION & PHOTO CREDITS

Illustration Credits

The publishers would like to thank the following two illustrators for their work on this book.

David Miller; 6, 12, 16, 20, 24, 28, 32, 36, 40, 64, 68, 72, 100, 104-5, 106, 114, 118, 122, 126, 130, 134, 138, 142, 146, 150, 154-5, 164, 168, 172, 176, 184, 192, 196, 204, 208, 212.

Mick Loates; 10-11, 44, 48, 52, 56, 60, 76, 80, 84, 88, 92, 96, 110, 156, 160, 180, 188, 200, 216, 218.

Additional Illustration Credits

G.Mikel 13; Roger McPhail (from *The ABC of Fishing*); 17, 21, 25, 29, 33, 37, 41, 65, 69, 73, 101, 111, 115, 123, 143, 147, 150, 161, 165, 169, 177, 193, 209; Keith Linsell 43, 81; New York State Department of Environment and Conservation 49; Tom Dolan, 53; John Bailey 61, 127; www.life.umd.edu 83; www.bbmwd.org 89; www.thaifishingguide.com 93; www.fishinghurghada.com 107; www.dpi.nsw.gov.au 131; www.nicaraguafishing.com 135; www.landbigfish.com 119, 139; Henry Gilbey 189.

Photo Credits

The publishers would like to thank the following sources for their kind permission to reproduce the pictures in this book. All other pictures are © John Bailey.

iStock; 49, 50, 74, 81, 108, 119, 120, 121, 127, 128, 151, 152, 202; James Ellis; 58, 77, 78 (bottom); Simon Channing; 59, 93, 94, 95; Jim Tyree; 78 (top and middle); Neill Stephen; 98; Shirley Deterding; 107, 109; Akshay Malavi; 132; John Watson; 137; Henry Gilbey; 148, 149, 189, 190; www.JohnRawlefishing.co.uk 214.

Every effort has been made to acknowledge correctly and contact the source and/or copyright holder of each picture, and Carlton Books Limited apologizes for any unintentional errors or omissions, which will be corrected in future editions of this book.